A Belief in the Miraculous

Buddhism, Magic,

and a Sense of the Sacred

by Jason Espada

A Belief in the Miraculous

Buddhism, Magic,

and a Sense of the Sacred

Great Circle Publications

ISBN # 978-1-948589-04-8

First Edition, January, 2018

For information contact: jasonespada.com

Preface

When I was in my 20's, I had the good fortune to study teachings from the Western Esoteric Tradition. These included, among other things, explanations of other levels of existence, psychic development, and systems of divination. Such teachings were very helpful to me back then, as the realities they spoke of were a close match to my own lived experience.

By the time I was in my late 20's, I had found my way to Buddhism, and to the Tibetan Tradition in particular. By comparison, holding the Western Esoteric teachings were like having a collection of well made and useful maps, but, for myself, in the Buddhist teachings I was able to sense more clearly how the different aspects of our life relate to each other, and to the whole. I especially appreciate how love and compassion is so clearly placed at the very center of all the teachings in Buddhism. At that point I shifted the emphasis of my study. The teachings on the uses of our subtle nature, and on the miraculous have never left me, however, and I've continued to put them to good use over the years, as may be sensed from this collection.

I recall one teaching from the Western Tradition that says there are two kinds of people when it comes to having the sensitivity to perceive more subtle realities: one is the naturally sensitive person, and that kind of person's challenge is to learn to control their experience; the other kind is less sensitive by nature, and that type of person has the challenge of increasing their awareness. I have always been the first type of person, so when I found my way to the Western teachings, it was a great relief. They were describing my world, and a way to live and not to have to struggle so much, but to flourish in it!

2 A Belief in the Miraculous

I thought to gather some writings from over the years and add a few Buddhist essays to this current collection for two reasons. First, I feel these ideas really do hold together well as a set, presenting a cohesive and practical world view, especially for people who are aware of energetic levels, and the miraculous. Second, these days, if a person studies Buddhism here in the West, they would be hard pressed to see much if any description our subtle nature, and what can be done with it, of other worlds and beings, or a celebration of the divine help that can be called on. I offer this then as my own small contribution for those who are interested in subjects such as these.

May whoever this finds its way to
enjoy peace and ease,
and delight in the riches of our world
May they be able to skillfully access the resources
that are always available to us all
for their own benefit
and for the benefit of their loved ones,
family and friends,
and for all beings

Table of Contents

4 A Belief in the Miraculous

6 A Belief in the Miraculous

8 A Belief in the Miraculous

The Light that is still with us

{I hesitate a bit to write this one, but... I have to at least try...}
There's a teaching I remember hearing called, 'What we talk about' – let me see if can get this right. I think it goes something like this, that:

The best things in life we don't talk about because there are no words for them. We don't even try to wrap language and ideas around those things, maybe because they are too big, or so extraordinary, such that we don't have even the idea of trying to say it.

Then, the next best things, the really good things in life, we have thoughts about, but we keep them to ourselves. These are most personal, and so close to ourselves and our experience that we wouldn't want them to be misunderstood or not appreciated, should we utter a word about them.

Poetry sometimes can stand at the border of what language can say, and, rather than try to encompass, it points the way, and is inviting...

For example, Rumi says,

This is love:
to fly towards a secret sky,
and to cause hundreds of veils to fall away,
moment by moment...

{As with many of his poems, this one ends with the sense of a hushed silence, and wonder...}

And so then, what we're left with when it comes to our everyday language, is... everything else that we talk about. Ha! And so it is with wanting to write about the miraculous in our lives. I'm reduced to this – to try to use ordinary talk to refer to something that is not ordinary at all. It's like holding nothing but simple clay in my hands, and wanting to represent something magnificent. What can I do? But something should said, or at least referred to, I'm thinking, from time to time.

(This is me riding on part of my 'hurry up and say it' motivation, that I've been feeling lately, which is essentially touching the truth of impermanence here on this beautiful earth, with my beautiful family and friends, and feeling, because of that, like we all have this chance to live fully, and that we shouldn't hold anything back at all.

This idea, of our just being here briefly, and that none of us know just for sure how long we have, makes deciding to do some things, such as to write, or to retreat, so easy as to be effortless in a way. This activity depends on that realization, clearly, and so, here goes...)

I think part of the reason why something so extra-ordinary that we would call it miraculous is not talked about often, is because as human beings we are so apt to dis-believe. This is nothing new – we can find teaching stories on this theme throughout time in great traditions, both East and West.

I had to laugh when I heard the one about the Israelites complaining when they were in the desert, and were criticizing Moses and God. After all, it was pointed out, their Lord had recently parted the Red Sea for them to escape from the hand of Egypt. Now, can you imagine having lived through an event like that and later complaining? Incredible!, but like all good teaching stories there is a truth being vividly expressed there about all of us human beings. It was the same way, apparently, with the disciples of Jesus – after witnessing so many miracles, still they doubted! Can you imagine?

At one time, I liked to remind myself, as a way to keep an eye on my so so frequent disbelief in what I was seeing, that, 'the problem is, that a miracle happens on Monday, and on Tuesday we forget about it!' (and now I would add: 'and complain too!')

This kind of thing happened also in the Buddha's time. Apparently one of his monks was demonstrating various powers, and was chastised by the Buddha, or so the recorded version of it goes. The Buddha then officially forbade them from showing psychic powers unless there was a good reason for it. One can only imagine a great being like the Buddha, perhaps levitating or moving through solid objects (like one of his modern day followers, Dipa Ma, is said to have done).

The Buddha had so much to teach people, the greatest gifts, but I'm sure that many in the crowds went away talking only about the extraordinary things they had seen, and maybe debating whether they were real or not, and then returning the next day, and, instead of wanting to hear teachings on liberation and enlightenment, only wanting and maybe calling out loudly for some unusual demonstration. One can only imagine the Buddha getting wise real quick to the drawback of showing what he and enlightened beings could do, or even talking much about it.

Still, there are miraculous things happening in our lives, and it's to our great advantage to know this and to remember when this has been so, because I'm sure that same power is with us even now.

We forget, I know, I know, and I know, and, it's such a loss!
The same power that has answered our prayers before is still with us;
    we can verify this for ourselves
    that power that helped us get through the hardest of times is with us,
    that power that brought unexpected success,
    that made a way out of no way,
    the power that parted the Red Sea,

the power that raised Jesus from the dead,
that appeared as light, when we needed it most,
and that, for a time to our perceptions, validated our faith with visible results…

Now, I don't know for sure what to call such a power, except perhaps… Grace… other people may call it different things, and, indeed, the power that works like this has been given many names, and as far as I'm concerned, all of them are true names to the people that hold them close. Names are not important, but what the names point to is most important.

This doesn't suppose much, or any of a belief system – it's reference is to something much closer in our lives than that. Grand, over-arching theories are not really of much concern or help when we're in trouble and fighting for our lives.

I suppose this is to say I have faith in a higher power, or in something much greater than I now understand. Maybe some day I'll understand it completely, and I'll be sure to come back and tell you all about it when I do, but, for now, this is the truth of it.

The faith that I have brings greater peace, when things are uncertain, or scary. This is part of how it works: when I remember the past, and how things worked out because of the light and power that was there, I know that it helps me to touch the truth of its being present also now.

Faith also seems to open the way for the energy of grace to come into our lives. It's always there, I trust, but, from our side, if we have this much trust, I've seen, for some reason, that it helps to bring that power through. I can't say why this is so, but I can say that I've seen this at work over the years, and so I feel like I have to at least try to say it.

When we're feeling particularly faith-less, it isn't that this power is not there, but we may not notice its presence, rely on it, or take advantage of it.

When we look, when we even celebrate the good we've received somehow in this life, it makes the actual presence of that grace more clear to our mind now. They say we should give thanks regularly to God, and if we think that way, I can see its point.

If we're not of the habit of thinking Theistically, still there is so much we have to be grateful for, and so much help we've received from outside, and in our lives, however we like to think about it.

I think that gratitude and thanksgiving, praise and celebration of all we've received in the past has a valid, and truly vital role to play in our seeing and accessing the blessings for our lives that are available now, today, however we like to think of them.

It's like we're thirsty, regularly, really needing water to survive and thrive, and there is a stream of fresh water running close by, within reach, just a few feet from where we are. It may be there, but if we don't see it, we can't get its benefits. Regular thanksgiving, praise and celebration are skillful ways to keep in mind that something very much like 'a stream of fresh water to a thirsty person', has helped us in extraordinary ways in the past, and these are ways that help us to see its presence in our lives now.

I don't know what others will make of this, but I felt that, at least once in a while, something like this needs to be said.

Grace and Buddhism

Grace is the power by which we are ultimately saved, and grace is the power we have to change. - Joyce Meyers

I've always admired the concept of grace in Christianity. I've marveled at the beauty of it, and how it describes a real, profoundly transformative event in people's lives. Such a wonderful thing, they are describing!

Sometimes I've felt like it is present in Buddhism also, for example, when I think of the blessings of the Buddhas and Bodhisattvas, the Saints and our teachers, and the Dharma, and the love we have received from our parents. Nothing we could have done could have 'earn' this kindness. It is a tremendous thing. And, just as a blessing is described in Christianity and in other religions, it has the power to 'tip the scales', so to speak.

I remember the title of one book of Beat poetry called 'Grace beats karma'. When I saw that I had to laugh, because in Buddhism we don't usually speak in these terms. In Eastern Traditions, it is talked about, with such terms as 'darshan' (the blessing of being in the presence of a Teacher), and 'shaktipat' (a transmission of spiritual energy), but I've not heard grace mentioned in the same way by Buddhist teachers, or in books on Buddhism. In Buddhism, as it has reached these shores up to now, it's usually all very mathematical, with the teachings about karma saying that this action produces these precise results. This may have some truth to it, but when it comes to our lives, and the possibilities that exist, especially when we connect with a spiritual tradition or teacher, more needs to be said.

When we are blessed by something or someone, we really have to throw out our calculators. There is no way to measure the great positive influence of a Sage or a Savior in our lives. This is spoken of in many great traditions.

Grace is described in Christianity as 'God's free and unmerited favor'. Interpreted in non-theistic language, this has its equivalent for us also in a very practical and accessible way, in our own Buddha Nature, that which is with us all the time. This profound truth of our nature is described in the literature as unproduced by our efforts, unblemished, beyond delusion, and, as it is, the source of all good qualities.

This is our 'original, unborn, and undying wisdom, which radiates all the time', says Khenpo Palden Sherab Rinpoche.

He says,

'This is the most powerful light. At this moment, the undying flame of wisdom is hidden behind or within our phenomenal conceptions. This inner light resides within us, never dimming, never losing its qualities, never dying out.

'Whatever brightness, clarity, analytic energy, or understanding we have actually arise from that original, unborn wisdom. All are none other than the innate nature of our own mind.'

This fundamental nature, that is beyond the reach of all deluded activity and mistaken concepts, is in us all. It is all of our birthright– and surely this fits any definition as a grace and blessing to each and every one of us! This potential we have is to really something to celebrate! This is what we aim to realize, both in the sense of understanding it, and in the sense of bringing its intrinsic good qualities to fruition in our lives.

Three parallels

There's always a risk when we compare great traditions that we'll oversimplify their message, or bend what they teach to fit what we'd like them to say. It is useful though, to compare teachings when they shine a light on each other, and complement the understanding and practice of each approach.

That said, here are three parallels I've found for grace in the Christian and Buddhist traditions. It seems to me that they are using different language to talk about the same thing – in very different frameworks, yes, but there you go. The 'active ingredient', I'm thinking here, is the same in both cases.

First, these two – the divine, or God's grace within, and our fundamental nature of mind, or Buddha Nature are with us all the time. The reality that 'The Kingdom of God is within you' was not just being invented as it was spoken by Jesus – it was the truth that has always been that was being pointed out by Him. This is a teaching on universal truth, and not just for those He was addressing. This is saying something about what is always and everywhere true. Quite radically different than how we usually perceive things to be!, and so it needs to be said, and experienced.

The same message, in Buddhist terms is that our fundamental nature is always with us, unchanging, and pure from the beginning. In the Treatise on Buddha Nature, by Maitreya, the basic teaching is this:

The essence of buddhahood abides within all beings,
obstructed by the stains of transient delusions.

The second idea is that receiving, and awakening to Grace, or the realization of this fundamental nature within us can be seen as the starting point for us in our spiritual practice.

In Christianity, it is in receiving Christ that our new life begins: *'You have taken off your old self, with its practices, and have put on the new self, which is being renewed in knowledge of its creator. Here there is no Greek or Jew, barbarian, Scythian, slave or free, but Christ is all and is in all.'* (Colossians 3:9-11)

In Zen, having an insight into our deeper nature is called satori. In the Nyingma and Kagyud schools of Tibetan Buddhism, this is called having the realization of the nature of mind. From that point, there is a re-orientation of practice. It's as if the clouds had parted, temporarily, and we're able to adjust our sense of where we are, and where we're heading.

Tho it's not often referenced, in the Nyingma, or Early School, they say that until we have a glimpse of the View, we don't really know what we're doing or where we're going in meditation. The same idea, in Christian language is that meeting Christ, from that point on, gives a new perspective on everything in life.

The third idea that I find in both Christianity and Buddhism regarding grace is the idea that this is what we draw from for our whole lives.

As one of my favorite modern Christian teachers, Joyce Meyer says,

'Grace is more than just the power to save us, it is the power we need for every single thing that we do.'

and,

'Here's what grace is: grace is not just the undeserved favor of God – grace is the power of the Holy Spirit, coming to us, freely, to help u to do whatever we need to do, with ease.'

The Scriptures say,

'Divine power has given us everything we need for life and godliness' (2 Peter, 1:3)

In the Christian tradition they make the distinction between what they call 'works of the flesh' and 'works of the spirit'. They sound the cautionary note:

'Unless the Lord builds the house, they labour in vain that build it'

And yet, if we look closely, there is also something blissful about this:

In Romans, it says

'Grace is a work that is done entirely with God's mercy, and without human effort.'

When this kind of power is present in our life, we can understand what the poet Rumi meant when he said:

'Stop swimming so hard,
and climb into the boat
with Noah...'

How excellent!

In one of his letters, it's true, Paul says he struggles, but that he does so using the grace he's been given.

'To this end I labor, struggling with all his energy, which so powerfully works in me.' (Colossians, 1:29)

In his book, The Glorious Pursuit, author Gary Thomas highlights that, *'Paul is laboring. But he is struggling with God's energy, not his own, 'which so powerfully works' within him.'* Elsewhere in the Gospel, Paul affirms that, *'I can do all things, through Christ, who strengthens me...'*

In Mahayana Buddhism, practice is framed in terms of what are called The Six Perfections: of Generosity, Ethics, Patience, Effort, Meditation and Wisdom, and it's taught that the true, natural, and, in a way, effortless expression of these all depend on Wisdom – which is insight into Reality, or our Fundamental Nature.

The Zen Ancestor Dogen referred to this at the end of one of his fascicles where he says, *'The treasure house opens, and we use it as we will...'*

In Tibetan Vajrayana Buddhism also, where they use visualization, this same idea is referenced when they say that the view is the necessary basis for all the prayers and practices that they do. Furthermore, there is an emphasis on the teacher-student relationship, and the blessings that are given and received through devotion form an integral part of practice within this living tradition.

Often when two traditions are compared, something is lost in the translation, or in the attempt to make things 'fit'. Hopefully that's not the case here. If, in drawing these parallels, what's at work in these traditions is any more clear, then I'll be glad. May that be to the benefit of all practitioners everywhere, and to all beings.

'Grace and peace be multiplied to you...'

I have this wish, for all of us, whoever we are, wherever we are. In the words of Timothy, and then Paul: Dear friends,

'Stir up the Gift that is in thee...'

and,

'Like good stewards of the manifold grace of God, serve one another with whatever gift each of you has received.'

Aah, how wonderful!

A few thoughts on faith and devotion

{these are few selections from essays I've written this last year}

For my own purposes, over the years I've come to view faith as an intuition, the knowledge of things not yet proven.

When it comes to faith, if anyone were to ask us how we know some things, or why we are being led to go in a certain direction, there's no answer we can give them that can satisfy either ourselves, or them, but without some amount of faith, our progress will be slow, or non existent.

One of the nice things about getting older is that we can look back on our lives, and, it gets easier to trust our intuition. We can look at times when we knew, without knowing how we knew, and followed that, and only later saw that things worked out, that there was something that matched the feeling we had.

'Faith goes into the spiritual realm, and brings out those things that are already there, where they can be seen.' – Joyce Meyer

If we have faith, we relax on some level. I think of those who are somehow cut off from this faculty, and how they suffer from wanting to know everything in advance. We know with our hearts so much more than can be understood with the intellect.

Faith is also associated a with devotion. If faith is trust and reliance, relaxing and believing in something, then devotion acts more like a magnet, drawing what we are devoted to us.
Khenpo Palden Sherab Rinpoche has these beautiful and true things to say about devotion: *'Devotion creates readiness, just as in the Spring the sun and rain make gardens ready to plant seeds and start growth.*

'Devotion is the key that opens the door of pure vision. It leads us beyond darkness, doubt and hesitation; it will help us recover from periods of difficulty. Devotion takes us beyond conceptions to an understanding of the true nature.'

If we follow our heart, follow our intuition, with faith, trust and devotion, then we will be led to paths we would never find otherwise, to depth and meaning and fulfillment. This is the ideal.

What we call faith is reflection of the mythic, poetic, and imaginative in us; the ability to have a vision, and to dream; it is linked with the Dionysian, ecstatic, and celebratory...

II.

Part of the problem for us Westerners is our over-reliance on rational thinking. This function has its place, but there are also some things that come to us only through the door of the love, the door of the heart, through faith and intuition, or direct experience. If we rely too much on the intellect here, it blocks us. When we want to know everything ahead of time, or have a logical explanation for everything, we can get in our own way.

I've thought of one analogy to describe both what's true about the rational view and also what it leaves out. It is: a black and white photograph of a color scene - it's true as far as it goes, but, there are many elements that are not seen.

Many spiritual truths don't lend themselves to being contained within concepts, and those who live just in the intellect suffer the loss of so many things, like the perception of beauty, mystery, wonder, intuition, inspiration and delight... These things are seen with the eyes of the spirit, and not with the eyes of the intellect alone.

III.

Ideally, faith, and our critical faculties can compliment each other. When faith is balanced with learning, it tests what we know, as much as we possible. Reason can then be used to highlight, and bring into application those things that are sensed with the intuition.

And when our well developed reason sees that it can only go so far, and that there is more that can be known directly, reason bows to faith and devotion, stands aside, and lets this ability fulfill its function.

Faith in Universal Goodness

I have faith in a universal goodness pervading all of life. I say this because I've had glimpses of it – timeless, endlessly inventive, and, when we see it, familiar to us all.

That this fundamental nature gets covered over, and our original impulse gets distorted accounts for a lot of our history, both personal and collective, but our story is also one of struggle against everything that follows from this basic ignorance.

Light breaks through in one person, then a group, and in a movement. We keep awake in the re-telling of these stories, and in the re-tracing of our history.

This week I learned about Seva – an organization dedicated to addressing treatable blindness worldwide, and I had to ask myself again, 'Is it true that thousands of people could be helped to see again, except that they are not known about, and not cared about?'

There are so many things here that we spend our time, energy, income and resources of creativity on – sports, computer games, clothes, food and drink, entertainments – the list could go on and on…

It feels to me like this is one more area that shows just how caught we are here, as a culture, as a people, bound up in our own problems to the exclusion of our family, our neighbor. There are many we could easily help, in extraordinary ways, were we free enough inside to respond to their needs.

I have no doubt that what covers our fundamental goodness also keeps us, every day we are here, from knowing and responding to the greater world, and the lives of our greater family.

It is natural to love, to give of our time, energy, creativity, encouragement and happiness. This all follows as a matter of course when we ourselves are sane, whole, balanced individuals, free of neurosis, and free of affliction.

However we formulate the path of such a mature person, it seems there's always some problem or other with it. For example, if we set the aim of a spiritually mature life as 'socially engaged, enlightened activity', we may not do the necessary inner work. We can instead take on a 'spiritual ego', or a helper persona, and while this has some value, it only goes so far.

If the inner work isn't done, at the very least, we've limited our own capacity. Worse still, the standard corruptions of human nature being what they are, if not dealt with individually, will again surface in whatever group or person comes into power.

And perhaps the biggest drawback to not deeply clarifying an essential human path for ourselves is that we really don't get to the root cause of manifold problems. That's one side of it.

On the other hand, if we take as the aim of human life and inner development just the personal freedom from suffering and limitation, then we have a definition that stops short of describing the subsequent outward, engaged aspect of a liberated life. We need both parts of a definition of a complete life – the inner development, and its communal expression.

Lama Yeshe said, 'We don't need to be enlightened before we can begin to act', and the thought from Gandhi, that whatever we do will be small, but it's essential that we do it - feels true here. But then seeing our limitation, and how much remains to be done should act as further encouragement for us to free ourselves. When the obscurations are cleared away, then our capacity to respond is fully awakened.

When I get down looking at our suffering world, and the neglect of those who could be doing more to help, I know I need to remember this – that the nature of us all is fundamental goodness, and that there are reasons for how we respond. Beneath the diverse views and actions, right along with all the troubles, I can see there is This is where I find my rest.

The Characteristics of the Pure Land
That is Always Available

I've been reflecting lately on the concept of Paradise, or a Pure Land. Although I've had these thoughts before, every time they come back around I am a bit surprised. When I go over this carefully in my mind, two things stand out that catch my attention whenever I think of it.

The **first** is that everywhere you read or talk to people, the concepts of Paradise are very consistent. Among people in different places and times and traditions, we hear a lot of the same descriptions. It is as if we have a collective idea of what a Pure Land, or Heaven, or a Paradise is - more on that in a moment.

The **second** thought that occurs to me whenever I think of this, and that always surprises me is that the Pure Land is available now. There is also sadness and astonishment that we don't always take advantage of this fact – that the Pure Land, Paradise, or Heaven is within reach. Mostly though, when I begin these reflections, I think of the characteristics of this Pure Land that is available to us all.

Some of the characteristics of the Pure Land, Paradise, or the Heavenly Realm, across cultures, and throughout time, are:

Space – there is plenty of space to walk around
Light
Beauty, like a garden, perfect
Great Peace
Perfection
Comfort and safety
and then,
There is no feeling of time in any conception of Heaven

There is no hurry in any description of Paradise that I know of, or can conceive of. There is no place to go – we have *arrived*. In fact, there is no feeling of time, as we know it, in the Pure Land. There, we are never late for an appointment, or feeling 'pressed for time', or like we have to hurry to enjoy ourselves because time is running out. Instead, there is the sense of limitless time available. This is consistently found in the idea of a Heavenly realm – it even feels familiar. There is the feeling of having plenty of time, and so there is comfort, well-being.

There is always joy in the Pure Land. Peace, yes, but also, always joy. Think about it.

There is no strife, no sadness, no suffering, no disease, no death, not even the words; no fear, no loneliness, or lack.

I was looking for a word or a phrase to describe the opposite of stress, with all its detrimental effects, and I thought of 'peaceful joy that is nourishing'. That is the experience of the Pure Land.

Often there is the feeling of Companionship there too, in thoughts of a Paradise. We feel loved there, known, and cared for, intimately, ultimately, forgiven, healed, made whole…

The Sun in the sky of the Pure Land – this is a life-giving vision.

Paradise, Heaven, is always described as feeling like we have arrived, as feeling like home. It is always a place, or an experience of great beauty, and perfection. These are some of the things that are always present in people's concepts of Paradise, or a Pure Land.

In my own concept, I think there is virtue and holiness there. People are not just 'hanging out', 'chillin', or partying, though on a higher octave, and they are certainly not engaged in any wrong or harmful actions. Rather, people or beings are engaged in virtue, and that is the cause of their joy.

We might say that this place is peopled with angels, or shining beings acting in angelic ways. This 'realm', so to speak, is available as a blessing to the world.

And there is praise, naturally. Paradise, or the Pure Land is a place naturally of songs, the music of the spheres, and feasts, and celebration; great harmony, friendship, music and dance... spontaneous celebration and delight...

Perhaps this is a metaphor though, saying 'it is like this'. When I think of a Pure Land, or Paradise, mostly the feeling I have is one of quiescence, of light and space. But these qualities are there as well - the richness, celebration, and healing; positive, generative qualities.

Of course, Paradise is also a place of awareness – if we sleep through it, somehow it would be less. *It is a place of awakening*, with the knowledge of beauty, and nourishing peace and joy.

Point Two – The Pure Land is Always Available

No Need for Thirst When Fresh Water is Within Reach

Isn't it remarkable that we have this expression – we say something is 'heaven on earth'? The connotation here, of course, is of some experience, far beyond the ordinary, that is all too rare, and all too brief. Naturally, it begs the question – how can we have more of that Pure Land, or Paradise kind of experience? The bliss, the peace, and the joy of it? It seems it should be possible...

I recall reading in An Autobiography of A Yogi, by Swami Yogananda, where he recounts meeting a woman Saint of his time, named Ananda Mayi-ma. I remember he described waiting for her to come out of meditation, and then saying that, she opened her eyes, 'refreshed from her dip in the infinite'. For some reason this phrase has stayed with me all these many years. I think if we asked them whether saints have anything that ordinary people don't have, they would answer no, and tell us that we all have the same resource available to us. This is at once a tragedy, and the best possible news.

If what they are saying is true, that the Pure Land is available, and we have not taken advantage of it, not only is that a tragedy, I would say that it is the forerunner of all other tragedies. It is the original fall from the Garden. Equally important though, as some sort of cosmic balance to our loss, is hearing that the experience of intrinsic freedom and joy is possible. How can this balance our great, mythic loss? I am an optimist, but, surely, this presages every other lasting happiness, and here is why: In spite of our grievously long exile, and imagining our selves so poor, yet there is a jewel sewn into the hem of our garment, as the old folktale tells. It is immutably available.

'It is not more in Buddhas, not less in ordinary beings'.

It's about here that traditional teachings like this begin to make sense: Huineng said: "When one has realized one's True self/ mind/ buddha nature, then all sentient beings are Buddhas. But if one loses one's True self/ mind/ buddha nature, then all Buddhas are sentient beings." True cultivator of Dharma, see not the fault of the World!" Pretty straightforward, isn't it?

The proposition is that the Pure Land pervades and transcends all experience; and that it is not dependent on conditions. It is changeless, and in some ways unchange-able – it is always available. There is nothing we can do to improve this Naturally Existent Perfection, but there are things we can do to facilitate our experiencing it, just as there are things we can do to block or obstruct our knowing this, experiencing this, and dwelling there.

I remember Joseph Campbell quoted a line from the Gnostic Gospels that said something like: 'The Kingdom of God is spread upon the earth, but men do not see it'. And I thought, now, why is that? Why, if all this beauty and perfection is available, peace, richness, and light, then why don't we know it?

In a talk on walking meditation, Thich Nhat Hanh said the following:

'...Suppose I have a miraculous power - I would like to bring you to the Pure Land of Amida Buddha, or, if you are Christians, the Kingdom of God. But once we are there, how shall we walk? Shall we print our sorrows and anxiety on the Land of Amida Buddha? That way we will pollute the Pure Land, and the Pure Land will become impure. Therefore, it's very important that we can make peaceful, happy steps right here on earth...'

I think he is saying that even if we are in this perfect a place, if we bring our anger and fear, then we won't experience it as perfect and pure. To enter Paradise, we would need to leave aside our anger, despair, fear, restlessness. In other words, as much as possible, we need to have a pure mind ourselves, and we need to touch this world deeply. Then our experience is altogether different.

I remember on retreat once Thay said, *'When you touch deeply the historical dimension, you reach the ultimate dimension, and when you reach the ultimate dimension, you have not left the historical dimension.'* He also said *'When you touch the ultimate dimension, you get the greatest relief'.* The Ultimate Dimension is another name for the Pure Land, as is Nibbana, - the extinction of suffering, the extinction of defilements.

Thich Nhat Hanh continues:

'...And as you can make peaceful happy steps on the earth, the earth becomes the Pure Land. And that is something I did not invent - that is said by the Buddha Himself. The Pure Land is in our mind.

Also the samsaric world is in our mind. It depends on our way of making steps that this land is a Pure Land or the samsaric land...'

Think how it is with beauty: some people see it and some don't. Beauty needs a pure subject, we could say, to reflect it fully. If our mind is cloudy, or dull, or not able to know, then that beauty, or joy, will not be experienced. If a person is deluded, or afflicted, or not present; scattered, or motivated to use, or exploit some landscape, or a painting, or a flower, then that mind itself is not reflecting what is here, but if we are present, and appreciative, then, oh such wonders can be known! they can be felt, they can be experienced.

Rumi says:

Make your loving clearer and clearer
No wantings, no anger. In that purity
you can receive and reflect the images of every moment,
from here, from the stars...

Oh, Look at the beauty of this world! Simply...open your eyes and look at the world – besides the misery, besides all that is tragic, lacking, or demanding our response – there is also a world of wonders that is here. This much is certain for me, and verifiable also, by anyone. The natural world, and the treasure of all the remarkable things people have made and have done; all the sublime tastes and all the things that are once-only-in-the-history-of-the-world... well, you get my point... this is a door... and we do so much need at least to 'visit', or to experience something of the Pure Land, and receive its' benefits, today, while we have such   great opportunity.

There is a common, inherited idea that Paradise, or Heaven is something we get after this world, but I don't sense the logic in that – especially since it's clear that 'wherever you go, there you are', eh?

Kabir says:

Friend, hope for the Guest while you are alive
Jump into experience while you are alive!
Think... and think... while you are alive.
What you call 'salvation' belongs to the time before death

If you don't break the ropes while you're alive
do you think
ghosts will do it after?

The idea that the soul will join with the ecstatic
just because the body is rotten -
that is all fantasy
What is found now is found then
If you find nothing now,
you will simply end up with an apartment in the City
of Death
If you know the Divine now
in the next life you will have the face of satisfied desire

We do need at least a glimpse, a brief, unmistakable opening, so that we have the Pure Land as a reference point. This poet also said:

Kabir saw this for fifteen seconds,
and it made him a servant for life...

I have a notion about such glimpses, as reference in our lives. Sometimes here in Northern California the coast will have quite a bit of fog move in, and, if you are driving, of course you have to take it slow. The image that I have, that I compare with having a glimpse of a Pure Land kind of experience, is like this: it's like driving and having the fog part for a minute, so we can see where we are, and where we should be headed.... then, even if, or when the clouds return, we will still have some sense of direction. It is imprinted on us, so that, even if we forget intellectually, on some deep level we remember, and are guided from that knowledge...

This is the Pure Land as a reference point. This is altogether different from our usual way of conceiving of ourselves and this world, and it is so necessary for us all. It is the truth that sustains us.

The Imperfect and the Beyond Perfect

On a personal and social levels, as a human being, there are some things we must resist, and work to change. None of us should accept unnecessary suffering in ourselves or in the world; none of us should accept injustice, or threats to our own and our children's shared world; and none of us should accept war, especially now, with modern nations' destructive capability. Even if it means thinking ahead several generations, merely by virtue of being a human being, we absolutely have to work, and struggle to keep from becoming numb, or complacent.

There is so much need. How then to live with ourselves, and with all that is unresolved?, and how to live in this world? Where will we get the energy to work? Do we need to turn our back on suffering to get what we need? It is right at this juncture that I find a saving grace – like - aha - this world is not as simple as our thinking would have us believe.

When we bring to mind pairs of words such as happiness and sadness, peace and war, satisfaction and dissatisfaction, contentment and discontent, it seems that such opposites cannot exist at the same time, but in fact they can and do co-exist, and exploring this paradox can yield riches.

I'm just about finished reading the psychologist Robert Johnson's book on contentment, which I've enjoyed, and which has led to these and a few other reflections.

When it comes to happiness, usually we think in either-or terms. We are either dissatisfied, or we are satisfied. We can't possibly be both, can we?

Last week I wrote out some thoughts about what I called 'neurotic dissatisfaction'. It is the kind of mind that cannot be satisfied, no matter how many possessions or different kinds of experience such a person has. It seems it's gotten more common in our culture, for young people especially to become more and more quickly jaded, burned out, sarcastic and disrespectful of just about everything. There is no happiness there, or satisfaction, or, it seems, the hope of satisfaction. It's a strange problem that needs profound work to change.

Just to be clear, when I refer to the possibility of being both satisfied and not satisfied at the same time, I'm not talking about the neurotically dissatisfied mind.

For people who are still capable of happiness, I realized that the things we are not and should not be happy with in life very much need the kinds of experience that 'have light to them'. These different experiences are available to us and they can and should co-exist in us. They may have to be experienced first one then the other, at times so we can take care of ourselves, but ultimately they shouldn't be kept separate.

I was thinking that the word 'contentment' doesn't go far enough when talking about the good; the word 'perfection' doesn't reach far enough either. There are some things that I think of as really being beyond perfection. What I mean is that sometimes, when we meet something great, with an open, fresh mind, the experience is more than we could ever have imagined it would be.

Our conceptual mind cannot begin to contain the beauty, richness, healing power, joy and nourishment of – say, for example, a cloudy morning, the wind, a friendship, kind parents, great teachers, the existence of music or the shades of color we call green.

Such things as the beauty of that child, and your smile, and so much more feed us; they sustain our souls and make them healthy and robust. When we put our mind entirely on such things, there is peace in meeting them, and we don't - we can't possibly ask anything more of them. How could I possibly ask anything more of a hummingbird? – I'm astonished – I realize I could never even begin to conceive of something like this.

These things have the feeling of being extraordinary gifts, so in that way we can say we are content with them. There is necessary peace to be found here. Such experiences are complete as they are, and what's more, they are overflowing, they move beyond themselves. They are life itself, and we all need to be in touch with these beyond-perfect things, for our own sake, for our family and friends sake, and for the sake of our communities and the greater world.

We each need nourishment, and nourishment is available. Maybe though the problem is that we haven't been taught to fully, rightly honor in our heart the sun, the wind, the earth, or friendships, arts, education, history or each other; maybe we haven't been taught to fully, rightly honor the miracle of our own eyesight, our breath, and motion…

Maybe we each need to learn how to be with these things quietly, in an unhurried way, and in an open-hearted way, so that we can receive their gifts. You can call it anything you like. Personally, I call it contemplation, but that's not quite it either for me. It's more like being with something and learning to be appreciative is being nourished by it. The joy of being alive is here.

Being in touch with the beautiful things, the life giving things is essential. Then, for everything else that life is, for all the 10,000 sorrows of the world, the benefit, the virtue of these gifts can continue. Real benefit can continue in places where it is needed most.

In Buddhist terms, when you see only the suffering of the world, with no apparent way out, that is called 'samsara'; when we see and experience only what is right, fine, pure, rich, unchanging, unmixed, undeluded, without affliction, peaceful, that is called 'nirvana'; and when you are able to see and experience both at the same time, that is called 'the realm of Buddha activity', and it's this last one, clearly, that this world needs more of.

One analogy for this is that we are able to hear two things at the same time, like music and a voice speaking, without the two obstructing each other in any way. They co-exist in our perception, and they can influence each other as well. So, for example, the quality of music (Mozart's Clarinet Concerto, slow movement) can influence how a mother asks her teenaged son to clean up his room; or two people in dialogue can each influence each other's tone and what is said. They interpenetrate and effect each other.

Buddha activity arises, we can say, from a base of something perfect, or, more accurately, beyond perfect. When in touch with suffering, compassion arises. We respond to this world out of a heart of love, for as long as is needed. This fundamental divine nature is touched by, and touches suffering, and is able to bring relief and transformation over time. That which is vast, and made of light both retains its' character, and at the same time is able to move, to touch, to influence, like light, like words, like rain. Now isn't that something?

Two Ways We Can Condition the Mind

It's become clear to me that there are two completely opposite ways we can use and condition our mind. One way leads to a contracted and deeply impoverished view of ourselves and our world, and the other leads to more expansiveness, and to a bright, blessed and enriched experience.

If we develop the habit of focusing on what is right about ourselves and this life, and being nourished by it, the world opens up for us. Miracles are found everywhere, whole worlds of possibilities make themselves known to us, along with the energy to accomplish great things, both seen and not seen to the outside world.

If instead we develop the ingrained habit of focusing overwhelmingly on what is tragic, or distorted, or far from the expression of our true human nature, over time we lose the sense of the miraculous. We can become jaded and numb, with senses obscured, isolated from each other and the natural world. The resulting experience is then one of fear, aggression and despair. There is a marked absence of light, joy and peace – all the things any healthy person would want for themselves.

There is a way to celebrate our being here, and to hold and care for the difficult aspects of our personal and shared life, and it is that very skill that we need to learn and to practice most of all.

A heart and a mind that treats self and others and this earth with reverence is plainly the result of learning to see things as they are, with breadth and depth and clarity of insight. The arts, our loved ones, our ancestry and Traditions, our natural world, all these are abundant sources of joy and fresh inspiration. With gratitude, meditation, quieting ourselves, prayer, ritual, and study, and structuring our lives to refresh ourselves as needed, we can access these gifts more and more.

The result is joy and strength, optimism and courage, and life lived with delight, as it should be. As we learn the art of healing ourselves and our world with all these means, we find more within our reach, and we tell our neighbors, friends and family, using universal language.

I have written this in response to the way this world is now, in response to how we are currently using our precious lives, played out against the unchanging background of our possibilities for health and happiness.

Joy and The Emotion Body

There is a description of what makes up a person in the Western Esoteric Tradition that I've found useful over the years, and that I'd like to draw out one part of as it relates to joy, and making progress on the path to being a complete human being. The teaching I'm thinking of here is usually referred to as 'the different bodies of a person'.

In brief, these are the physical body we're all familiar with, followed by a more subtle energy body, sometimes called the etheric body. More subtle than this is the astral body, which can be divided, for the sake of talking about it, and for practical purposes, into the lower astral, or emotional body, and the higher astral, or mental body. More subtle than these are the subtle mental body, and then the spiritual body.

You may have seen diagrams of a human form, with layers around it, symbolizing these different bodies. If the picture is in color, then these 'sheaths' will have different colors as well. The 'bodies' actually all interpenetrate, even if they are shown, for teaching purposes, in this way.

We are all familiar with these elements of our life, even if we haven't given them these names. They are what make up our experience of ourselves.

Where language that names them, and traditions of study and working with these aspects of ourselves are useful, is that they offer perspectives on ways of self development that may be lacking, or not articulated as well and fully in other traditions. I think this is the case with the Western teachings on the emotional body.

A few more signs of the emotional body

The state of a person's emotional body can actually be heard in their voice. This is something we all know, but maybe haven't had it framed this way before. Whether someone's feeling well, or is upset, if they're self confident, or anxious, insecure, or disconnected, this is something that communicates through the sound of their voice.

At times, a sensitive person can pick up on the feeling tone of how a person sees themself, and the main tenor of their habitual moods. There's nothing surprising about this, because we all live in this ocean of communicating with each other, not only through words, but more importantly through the timbre, and the cadence of how we express ourselves.

When we're having a conversation, for example, we can tell if we're being understood, or if we're having the effect we wish to have, such as calming a person, by picking up on the subtle changes of inflection in their voice. Happiness can also be heard, and this is the resonance of the emotional body we hear.

One of the central ideas in both Western, and Eastern Esoteric teachings on the different bodies is that the more subtle conditions, or influences the more gross body. So, for example, the energy body effects the physical; the emotional, the etheric; the level of more subtle mind effects the feeling body, and so on, up to the spiritual body of a person, which is the most influential of all. This kind of viewing things, and working, is called 'moving up the planes'.

One more feature of these teachings, useful here, is that energy can be blocked at any point, and so there is the need to identify and remove these blockages, for the sake of a good circulation of energy, for health and wholeness.

I've not seen very much written about emotion in Buddhism, so I thought I should say something about it, because healing, health, and development on the path, needs to include this part of ourself.

The key role of the feeling body

It's always interesting when we meet what feels like some barrier to progress, in cultivating the qualities we know we want to have more of in our life. Such has been the case with me, with knowing that I want to be capable of being aware of my own and other's sufferings, and to be able to respond to them well. So often, in the past, I've felt that the best I could do is meet the hurt or fear as best as I could, and try to take care of myself in the interim.

What I didn't realize is that we can increase our capacity to be with what is difficult to a very great extent, and that the key to this is the development of our ability to experience joy. I am sure now, more than ever, that this is something we under-utilize, and that, because of this, we're not as capable as we can be, of being in touch with our own hurts, or of being present, and reaching out to others in need. If we were to nourish ourselves as well as we could, and develop this capacity, there's no telling what we would be able to do.

It may be of use here to note that in Eastern Traditions, and especially in Buddhist psychology, there is no category for what we in the West call emotions. In their analysis, what we call emotion is the rapid interaction between thought, and sensation. If we slow down and watch our experience enough, we can see what they mean. There are times when a thought will come, without much feeling to it, say, of a person we're going to see later that day. If we catch it, and/or don't take that thought up, following it with other thoughts, it can subside, like a cloud disappearing back into a clear blue sky.

What often happens though, is that, consciously or semi-consciously, we add to this first thought, and begin to generate either pleasant or unpleasant feelings, such as craving, anger, or fear.

It can go in the other direction as well. A positive thought, given attention and added to, can produce a good feeling, or sensation, and, very clearly, this can be healing for us. The problem is that, for the average person, most of our 'cultivation' is not consciously chosen. We see ads, hear news reports, meet with other people who have problems and afflictive emotions, and, most of all, we continually follow our own ingrained habits of mind, which are often negative, self denigrating, and, after a time, self reinforcing.

To relate this to the Western teachings, take for example, just this simple description of the physical body, followed in subtlety by an energy body, and then feeling. We can watch how we react to both positive and negative thoughts and experiences throughout the day. Often, when things are too hard to hold in our experience, we'll find a way to shift to another level – either by going to the more gross level, eating something so as not to feel what's hard, or moving up to more the level of mind – 'taking our mind off of things' we'd call it. Actually, it's moving up, and away from the feeling, into thought or abstraction.

Sometimes this is good, and skillful, and sometimes less so. Sometimes, it can be a relief from feeling too much, to give it a rest, to take a walk, or go to a movie, to read a book, quiet our mind, or talk with a friend. This movement to take care of ourselves happens naturally, and it's appropriate at times to step back from the sense of what's going on, but when it becomes habitual, and when we don't know that there are other choices, the result can be that a person becomes detached from feeling, from knowing on that level either their own life, or what's going on in the lives of others around them.

The problem of not being able to feel is more than just this insensitivity, or a lack of awareness – to be more precise, it's the lack of ability to hold some things in consciousness. There are many good intentioned people who just are not able to be with suffering, either their own, or that of others. This is not a character flaw, I'm thinking, but the result of never being taught, and never practicing the ways we have available to us to become truly strong and capable beings.

We all know what's meant by someone 'shutting down' because of the experience or memory of something difficult, or painful, or dangerous. We often do this to ourselves, to some extent, maybe by watching tv, distracting ourselves one way or another, or by spacing out. The more extreme forms are when something happens that can't be integrated, and even feeling itself is perceived as just full of suffering, and avoided.

We store experiences in our bodies, taught Wilhelm Reich, and if these were painful, we may avoid feeling, or being in our physical body, and emotions, so as not to experience any more suffering. Some people even become alcoholics, or addicted to some other escape, just because they don't know any better way to relieve, or to heal the past.

I remember writing a note on one retreat in 1989 to the Vietnamese Buddhist teacher, Thich Nhat Hanh, asking him, 'Is there any place in mindful living for blocking out pain?' I was 29 at the time, and this was something I had struggled with for years up to that point: if a person is sensitive to beauty, to all that is good in the world, they are also open to the suffering, and it can be overwhelming.

Thay answered in the next day's talk that, when things are difficult, we just do the best we can, but the best time to practice and strengthen ourselves is in ordinary times, and when things are going well. I was, and remain grateful for his response. This planted the seeds for where I am now.

During the same period, Thay taught that:

'The blue sky, the flower, the river, the cloud, these things have a healing nature. If you allow yourself to be in touch with these healing elements, the wounds within your body and your mind will be healed. We should allow ourselves to be healed, and therefore, we should allow ourselves to be in the heart of life, which contains so many wonderful things, like the children, the flower, and so on...'

"The seeds in our consciousness can function like anti-bodies. What is important is that you continue to plant new seeds, the kind of seeds that are both refreshing and healing. And if you just do that, by practicing mindful living so that you can be in touch with the flower, with the cypress tree, with the fresh air, with the beautiful eyes of the children, then these seeds will be planted in yourself, and they will naturally take care of the seeds of your suffering. You don't even have to touch them. And that is something I think the practice of Buddhism can contribute to psychotherapy in the west."

I've learned that when we experience anything beautiful, and it touches us, it's connecting with the feeling body. We can feel ourselves becoming enriched by watching the changing colors of the sun reflecting on the snow, by listening to Mozart, by thinking about our wonderful children... and in so many other ways.

What we find is that we receive nourishment though positive, uplifting experiences that we don't receive in any other way. Think about it: the food we eat with appreciation, the love of family and friends, enjoying some degree of health and education, cherishing music and poetry, and the loveliness of the afternoon light, these are things that can fill and strengthen us. Then when we are well nourished on that feeling level, it's clear just how it reaches and enhances every other part of our life. It becomes apparent how nourishing ourselves with joy is essential for our health, and for our becoming mature, capable, and fulfilled.

I put this in the category of fundamental education – like learning to eat and drink. It's something we should be taught early on, and then practice our whole lives in taking care of both ourselves, and others.

Buddhism, Religion, and the Supernatural

Looked at in the light of eternity, some things are easier to approach. Whereas before, our view was too narrow, too taken up with the dynamics of our everyday lives, settling back even for a day, or half a day, opens a more expansive visa on this, our world.

In my twenties, I made a study of Western Esoteric Philosophy, mainly because the world view described there so matched my own experience. Different levels of existence, orders of conscious beings, and divine help that is always available – these were, and continue to be the day to day fabric of my life.

Now, a person discovers very early on when they are out of step with those around them. It's like when a child sees spirits, and assumes everyone else can too, until finding out one day, much to his surprise and dismay, that it is not so. From then on, of course, they lead a dual life – one they can share, and the other that is the world of their inner reality, they way they experience the world.

A person searches philosophies and religions not only to make their way out of confusion and suffering, but also to find some affirmation for their view of the world. If others do have the same view of life as we do, the thinking goes, maybe they also have some thoughts on what our aims should be, and how to make our way here.

The reference point when searching out a religion or a teacher is inside. It is unyielding, some would say stubborn – restless with a kind of divine dissatisfaction towards philosophies or view that don't cut it, impatient even to the point of not bothering to criticize.

This sense of what we really need is something I'm sure we all have, and it is a true compass. On some level we know, this is the most important guiding sense we have. Anything that threatens that, we move against with the force of our whole being.

To turn and face my fellow Buddhists, we do share this wonder, and a reverence for the Founder of our traditions, but each of us do also carry with us, and see the world through a very different world view. Perhaps some good can come from talking about these differences. This is not to assert the superiority of one over the other, or to proselytize, but to suggest other possibilities as far as looking at our lives here, and particularly at our spiritual life and practice.

In Buddhism, you have to look to the Tibetan Tradition to find a cosmology or world view similar to the Western Esoteric Tradition's understanding. This is not so much the aspect that is emphasized in that school's teachings, but it is the ground, the basis of their ideas and practices. Their overall view pervades everything we find there.

There are oracles, visions, the appeal to saints, and the receiving of blessings from one's teachers, Buddhas and Bodhisattvas. That aid and support to a person's spiritual life in this world are the daily bread and the nurturing ground in the Tibetan view. That this is curtly dismissed in the minds of many Westerners, as primitive, 'magical thinking' is a great loss, as far as I'm concerned.

From what I said earlier, it should be obvious why I feel this way, but here I'll say a bit more about it anyway.

I imagine that if a person in any time and place, endowed with the faculties of faith, intelligence, vigor and persistence, were to search for the truth, that he or she would very likely find it – or at least some level of truth that has been found by other seekers throughout time. There would be nothing surprising about that.

Now, whether we like it or not, and whether we are aware of it or not, those of us living today are all to some extent the products, intellectually, of the so called 'Enlightenment', that rejected a lot of superstition that needed to be cut away, but that at the same time negated the truths and methods of religion as well. What we were left then with is a mechanical world view, that clings to a part of the truth of things as being its entirety. More is left out of the rational, materialistic view than is included.

There were always, and continue to be now, artists, independent thinkers, mystics and religious, that could never subscribe to such a barren view as this, and yet we find ourselves situated with all the effects of the Enlightenment in our education, economics, media, psychology, and even in our religion.

I understand that, for someone not sensitive to the invisible world, what some people do in their prayer and ritual, with appeals to saints, angels and ancestors, would be at least non-sensical, or worse, an object of scorn. They look down on such people as immature, or fools, misguided, superstitious, or just plain ignorant, and, charitably, to be pitied.

From the other side of it though, those 'non-believers', or those without inner vision are blind, and they mislead others.

Who's to tell what's going on here? I have my own experiences and ideas and practices to guide me, but for others who may be wondering how to navigate these same straits – I'd suggest two things: the first is to aim, as much as possible, to have an open mind. This means having a mind that is capable of learning.

My second suggestion is to study, as much as you can, how other people have made sense of life in this world. This will, at least, help develop a tolerance for others views. At best, it will open you to a greater experience of this one life we share.

Which brings me to Western Buddhism today, and the way it is being transmitted and understood in America, circa 2013.

There is not yet a Buddhism here that includes the realities of other dimensions of existence, of Saints and Enlightened Beings. We can't quite borrow the Tibetan view, as much of their philosophy derives from the place they came from. Neither can we look entirely to Western religions because of elements that many, myself included, can't entirely accept. And yet realities, and people's experiences being what they are – that is, messy, but having their own logic to them – transcend systems of thoughts. So we do need to somehow accommodate these experiences, or we are the lesser for it.

I'm in the middle of reading a book called 'The Good Heart', which is His Holiness the Dalai Lama's explanation of Christian scripture. As I'm reading, two themes keep emerging for me. One is the saying that, 'truth is one, but people call it by different names'. The other thought I've been having is one the Dalai Lama has made reference to many times over the years, and, that is, that the Western Sources are closer at hand, and more accessible for most people here.

So where does that leave a Western Buddhist in the twenty-first century? Like many other people here, I have a great respect and admiration for the teachings of Jesus. And more than that even, I feel a natural closeness and devotion to Him, as a Bearer of Light, as one who sustains us through hard times; as a Healer, and True Guide. From what I can tell, He is not the only form of truth and help, as most Christian assert, but He is no less true, powerful, and holy because of that.

He is on my altar, right along side the Buddha, surrounded all around by the images of Saints, Buddhas and bodhisattvas. I know some purists would say, well, that's not Buddhism as the Founder taught it, and I don't want to argue, but, if enlightenment is the aim, then any way to get there is fair game, no? And if our purpose, as brought out in the Mahayana, is the benefit of all beings, then the vision of a world in which there are many enlightened beings is something to be celebrated as helping us to accomplish our aims.

I'm a big believer in the power of prayer as a way to open ourselves to receiving blessings, and as a way to help others. Prayer comes naturally for Christians, but less so for us Buddhists. At least, it's not talked about as much, and, I suspect, it's not something we avail ourselves of as much as we could. It need not be this way. As Ani Tenzin Palmo said, since help is available, then why not call on that help?

There is more to be said, but maybe this in enough to point in the general direction I think is missing and very much needed in today's world, with its problems, and Traditions, and sincere, open minded practitioners.

May all be well.
May all be blessed.
May whatever methods people take up,
swiftly and easily lead them all to the fulfillment of their aims.

Another Ghostly Tradition

I know that if I start to write about the dead tonight, I won't be able to sleep. They will come and crowd this space and press me into their service, asking me to say their names again slowly, and to tell something of how they come and what they want from us.

One of the first things I noticed on arriving in Taipei in the Spring of 1999 was that on every street, there were card tables set up outside of businesses, with flowers and fruit on plates, and incense and often a whole roast chicken. When I asked the owners of the school where I worked what these offerings were for, they said they were for the local spirits. And when I asked how many local spirits there were in Taipei, the two women talked about it in Mandarin for a minute, and one of them turned to me and said, 'Fourteen'.

I had not only arrived in a new place, I also entered a world where I knew almost nothing about what people believed. There were temples on almost every other street, with what looked like Buddha statues, but that also had bearded statues I later learned were Taoist deities. Apparently, one could ascend to the level of what they call a god by living an extraordinary life. Then they would become an object of adoration, someone who was supplicated in difficult times, and a refuge when the outside world offered none.

For example, Confucius was prayed to before a test. Parents and students alike would photocopy student IDs and leave them at the altar. Copious amounts of incense was burned, mostly at the Taoist, but also at the hybrid temples that seemed to be the norm. Other deities, such as the goddess Matsu, were prayed to for safe voyages, or for a safe pregnancy. The strangest time of year, though, and the one with the most ghostly activity was what they called Ghost

Month.

Now, there were some things you just didn't do in Taiwan, ever, such as whistle at night (which was sure to summon a ghost) and during ghost month, the list grew to include not swimming (some otherwise very reasonable people took this very seriously); not making any big change in life, such as getting married, or buying a house, or changing jobs. Apparently everything of any consequence is put on hold for that whole month, because, as I was told, the spirits could be disruptive.

Ghost month begins with an eerie rite they call 'opening the gates of hell'. The Anglicized translation, though, no doubt sounds worse than it is. True, spirits with accounts to settle are invited to come for their due, but ancestors are also thought to be closer at this time, and especially important to connect with.

Just in case you're thinking that this only happens off on some side streets, think again. I remember a huge metal barrel, at least six feet across, in front of a large, reputable bank. In it there was a scorching fire to receive offerings of incense and thick bundles of paper money. I was told that those with more to spend are expected to make a big public display of their piety. Anything less would mark them as unfilial, and a deep shame would be incurred. I asked someone if they actually believed in the effect of making offerings, and got a reply and a look that said at once, no, not really, but I'm not taking any chances.

Around this time I also came to hear about what they call Spirit Marriages. This is where someone on the other side is freed from the misery of not having found a partner in their life, by marriage to a person who is still living. The story goes that a ceremony such as a spirit marriage can often quell disturbances or right the finances or health of people in a family. Ghost month has its arc too. Toward the end, there's a public festival of guiding the spirits back to their abode, with promises of offerings and devotion.

If enough people believe something, there's certainly a wave that travels at you down the street. That much I can be sure of. For traditional people in Asia there is much more awareness of other dimensions, and the interplay between the spirit world, and this one. Most people feel completely comfortable consulting mediums, and connecting to and being sustained by family ancestors and noble souls is a part of almost every household.

From what I could see, the people in Taipei were much more comfortable casting their gaze into the deep, having intimations of answers, and holding the mystery of the unnamed in their workaday lives. On the other hand, we in America scorn what we can't hold and trade in openly. Impoverished in our senses, short of vocabulary for what matters, and blind to anything that doesn't reflect our own image back at us, to come back here is to enter a dark tunnel, where its just the light of remembrance that feeds us.

Heaven and Hell

I heard myself recently giving voice to a thought I've had for some time now – to the effect that the Hollywood depictions of evil and hell realms seem cartoonish to me, compared to the real thing. Walking home this evening, it seems now is the time to set down a story I've had in mind for years. The short version of it goes like this:

After walking for a long time, I came to a fork in the road, where someone was sitting on a chair, whittling away at a piece of wood. I asked him, where do these roads lead, and he said, that way leads to heaven, and that way to hell. Thinking to myself, well, that was easy, I headed down the road to heaven. After some time though, a question started to form in my mind, so I went back. The fellow was still there, and so I asked him, Are there other people who come this way? Yes, he said. And do they ask the same question and get the same answer you gave me? Yes to both. Well then, I asked, does anyone ever take the other road? The one to hell? and to my surprise again he said yes. Why would they do that, I asked, and he answered,

Well, if you take the path to heaven you may always wonder about the other road, and what it may bring, and you will feel divided about it. On the other hand, if you take the path leading to hell, and find your way to peace after all that, you'll never have any fear after that. You will have gone through the worst, and understood it.

In the short version of this story, I then go through hell, and learn its lessons.

In the longer version, first I say, ok, well, thank you very much for the information, but I'll take the way to heaven after all.

I go to the heavenly realms, and enjoy myself there thoroughly. Time passes as time does in these places, in an elongated fashion, so we can't really begin to compare them to hours, days, months and years here on earth. It's more relatable perhaps to say that heavenly experiences expand a person. We awaken in ways we didn't know were possible.

After some time in a relative sense though, new questions about hell begin to form. There is, after all, so much time and space to think over things. And so back I go for another round of conversation with the man at the crossroads.

The first thing I want to ask him is if I would lose the memory of heavenly worlds, if I ventured into those states of woe, and he said, the whole range of experiences would be yours, in that regard. Sometimes hell is forgetting entirely that any other world exists, or is possible. At other times, the torment comes from feeling that heaven is possible, but it seems tantalizing, and eternally out of reach.

Well then, are there others in hell? Again, he answered, there is the whole range of possibilities that can be classified as states of deprivation: at times, there are far too many others, sometimes they are all suffering too, and at other times it may seem you or your group are the only ones in struggle and difficulty; and at other times, there is no one anywhere, in any sight, memory, or imagination.

Ok then, I asked, is it possible to help others in hell? And at that point, for the first time, the watcher at the crossroads brightened up and said, yes, it is possible, but then it wouldn't be hell to you any more. It might be a suburb of hell, or somewhere on the outskirts, but once you start thinking like that, and accessing that as even *a possibility*, then it makes paths out of those states. Your understanding of the whole terrain shifts.

Catching the general drift of what he was communicating, I asked one more question, which was, can hell be seen from heaven?, and he smiled and said, from some parts of it. Ok then, I said, and headed down the other path.

I've learned enough about the heaven worlds to know that in a manner of speaking they are peopled with wise beings, effulgent, and capable of miraculous activity. They make a way where there is no way.

They would say to us, What use is medicine and training, if we keep ourselves from where there is suffering? This is what the medicine *is for*.

And, If you are going to speak to someone, it helps if you look like them, and if you know the weight and texture of what they are going through.

From what I've learned, the hell realms have a few features in common. One of the characteristics is that they all feel like there is no choice or control. If it felt like there was an end point, it would all somehow be tolerable, but the mind contracts, or implodes in such a state, and the ugly distortions it produces take many forms.

There is usually fear, and aggression, an oppressive sadness, desperation and a deep fatigue along with the feeling that there is simply no way out. These are the common characteristics.

Compared to people in the human realm, it's much harder to tame the mind of a hell being because such a mind is continually stirred up with hostility and paranoia; it is thickly veiled, and sees neither itself or others clearly, but creates these realms where it suffers.

Those that are called, angels, Buddhas and bodhisattvas work unceasingly to free innumerable beings from their experience of inferior states, and we get to know a small part of their activity by our being human, and struggling and suffering here. If our vision were to open even a little to the perception of other realms, we'd find the range of what beings experience expands as well. The wisdom and compassion of the Divine beings is inconceivable, is comprehensive, and it spontaneously works on every level to liberate beings from suffering and to bring them to – what are for them - as yet unimagined states of well being and peace.

Sacred Outlook - Seeing Beyond Ordinary Perception in Modern Culture, and American Buddhism

'Beware of confining yourself to a particular belief and denying all else, for much good would elude you – indeed, the knowledge of reality would elude you. Be in yourself for all forms of belief, for God (Truth) is too vast and tremendous to be restricted to one belief rather than another.' - Ibn 'Arabi

{I write this for myself, and my family; Here is the great 'what if it is so?'...}

So much of our pessimism and despair comes from the limited views we that hold of ourselves and this world that we live in. This is not entirely our own fault. It comes as well from our culture and upbringing.

We would expect that religions, such as Buddhism, would offer an alternative to the one dimensional world of consumerism and competition, and to the flat, affect-less life of scientific rationalism. Instead we find that Buddhism is often presented strictly as another philosophy, or just as psychology, and divorced from many of the elements that would classify it as a religion. This is understandable- to a point. Many people come to Eastern religions because Christianity and Judaism didn't work for them. And what's worse, they've had those teachings proselytized at them by arrogant, narrow minded fanatics.

We like to joke that many American Buddhists are in recovery from Western religion. For many, the straightforward, practical teachings on how to take care of our minds are of great appeal and benefit. This is all good, but, if this is all it is, there are some profound and precious things that are being left out of our understanding of ourselves, and our world and of Buddhist teachings.

One of the great things about these times is that we are able to look at how other people received and practiced these teachings. One thing we can notice is that the starting place for many other people, in other cultures and times, has been very different than our own.

In most places, Buddhism is a tradition that is alive with wonder, rich with the presence of the sacred, and with the guiding influence of Enlightened beings. Here are a couple of quotes from modern teachers: The first is by Ani Tenzin Palmo, a British born nun, ordained in the Tibetan Tradition. She says,

'We are not alone. This universe is full of Buddhas and Bodhisattvas who are on our side. And, as is known in all Buddhist countries, although it is not always emphasized in the West, we can pray to them.'

And Lama Zopa Rinpoche has said:

'You are not alone because all the time there are numberless buddhas and bodhisattvas surrounding you, loving you, guiding you, that is what they do....'

Now, if we compare this way of thinking to the general way people view themselves and this world, and the way that Buddhism is usually taught in the Theravada and Zen centers in America, there is a very great difference. One perspective says that we're pretty much on our own. Another perspective says that there are many enlightened beings we can call on, and that can help us. Now, suppose for a moment, What if this were so?

If this is true, as I think it is, then we've reduced our view of this world and ourselves, our traditions, and our options, and this is surely a great loss to us all. What we have when this is the case is a tradition that has been greatly dis-empowered, and therefore generations of students, and those they are connected with, are being deprived of very great benefit.

I recently heard an interview with Sister Joan Chittister, where she said that the maps we use are important, because they are what will be followed by future generations to make their way in the world.

My world is rich, but many modern day Buddhists don't share this view, and they explicitly or tacitly deny so much of our potential and possible experience. There are abundant resources available by which we can actualize our aims, and if these are not taken advantage of, then it's like going hungry, and having our whole family go hungry, while there are fields nearby that can satisfy those needs. It is such an unnecessary tragedy to not see this much.

Ani-la added that:

'This is not being theistic – this is being practical. If there's help out there, why not invoke that help?..

May we all be well and happy
May we all awaken to the blessings that are continually here for us!

In a rich world view, Saints, Buddhas, Enlightened Intelligence, Bodhisattvas, and Divine help are available. If we don't know this much, then what are we left with? – a string of doctrines, and we're on our own? No! Our lives, our world, our Traditions hold inconceivably so much more than that! And while it's true that not everyone can perceive these things, or has an affinity with thinking this way - this is how it is in the world - they should at least consider the possibility of help from these sources. And they should at least not dissuade others who can draw great benefit, solace and inspiration from the presence of enlightened beings in their world view.

Another thing that leads people to reject all religious views is that prayers or the methods used don't always work in the way they want them to. It's the truth that many factors are involved either in bringing a result, or when something does not work. Our lives have this inconceivable complexity to it, as much as we may want to over-simplify things. I can say with many others that the sum of it is beyond me. What then to do?

Where the methods, and the views they are based on enter into it, and I think the reason they shouldn't be rejected outright, but taken up where and when we can, is that they are born of our collective instinct for knowing, and for making things right in our lives. These are methods that have been reaffirmed in every generation. They are our inherited wisdom of what has worked in the past, very often beyond anything that was thought possible.

Let's look at this together. This is how it is in these times: the common, mundane perceptions we live with and pass around are really more accurately de-valued, degraded views, of ourselves, each other, and our world. This reaches these days, unfortunately, even into how religions traditions are taught and received.

I wrote this poem a few days ago:

A grey scale teacher
splashes his grey scale paint-views
onto everyone and everything
They are a danger!
There is no joy there,
no color,
little depth of feeling,
little or no poetry or wonder,
richness or inspiration
Deprived themselves,
they deprive others…

Part of the problem for us Westerners is our over-reliance on rational thinking. This function has its place, but there are also some things that only come to us through the door of the love, the door of the heart, through faith and intuition, or direct experience. If we rely too much on the intellect here, it blocks us.

I've thought that one analogy that works to describe both what's true about the rational view and what it leaves out is a black and white photograph of a color scene. It's true as far as it goes, but there are many elements that are not seen.

Another analogy I thought of is this:

If we look at an ocean through a pinhole,
what we see
is a pinhole's worth of the ocean
It's like this.

Many spiritual truths don't lend themselves to being contained within concepts, and those who live just in the intellect suffer the loss of so many things, like the perception of beauty, mystery, wonder, intuition, inspiration and delight... These things are seen with the eyes of the spirit, and not with the eyes of the intellect alone.

Another element that plays into a common, mundane view is our pride. Every tradition, and common sense too tell us that humility is necessary for learning. It would be one thing if we knew we were arrogant, but when even this much self knowledge is lacking, it's really hard to learn from our teachers, this world, and our deeper nature. This is related to our receptivity. We can say: great humility, great receptivity; small humility, small receptivity; and no humility, then no receptivity whatsoever...

From culture comes a self created world view, and self fulfilling prophecy {Here is a sketch of how de-valued, ordinary perceptions of ourselves and our world develop, and how they can be undone. Like any sketch, it leaves out many things, but hopes to catch enough of the essential structure of what's going on to communicate its message.}

We live in a culture and a time that is lacking in its sense of the sacred. Wherever the best of human values are not given enough attention, or where religious culture is mocked or ignored, and where a sense of the beautiful is overridden by the volume and quantity of meaningless things, then we become inwardly impoverished.

We live in grossly materialistic times, that deny of the existence of everything beyond the reach of our ordinary five senses. Be assured, this has not always been the case in other times and cultures.

We may pride ourselves on having gotten over what we haughtily call 'infantile' views, of a spiritual world, or any higher order than what the average person can see. We denigrate 'magical thinking' as naïve, uneducated, false and misleading. We're so proud of our reasoning and science, and we set that as the standard for everything.

Modern consumer culture then isolates people, and over time, the human connections we all need grow thin. We become suspicious of our neighbors and friends, and set apart from family. The prevalent perspective is actually nihilistic, life denying, a tragic distortion of who and what we are.

The views many of us have inherited, just by the fact of having been born here, are then reinforced by our emotional reactions, which are then reflected back to us as appearances that are colored or tainted by our own minds. If our mind is not dealt with skillfully, a patina can cover everything. What all this adds up to is a disempowered view of what it is to be alive, to be a human being in this precious world of ours.

Collective views are shared in mostly unnoticed ways. They are pervasive, and are the ground of our sense of the choices we have, for change or development, or to remedy the problems we face.

To counteract this perception, or rather, misperception, we should be able to recognize diminished values, and degraded views wherever they exist, in ourselves, our family and neighbors, and in the world, so that we can replace them with something truer, something ever closer to the ideal. At the very least, our religions traditions and philosophies should offer us an alternative to nihilism. Life is available, and someone should say it out loud.

To love is to begin to remember who we are

What is it that brings light back into our lives? What will cause us to see ourselves and our world as it really is? Where will we find strength for all we need to do, and vision, and grace? Everyone, no matter whether they are affiliated with a tradition or not, can love. It can be a love for family, for art, for nature, for our teachers, for our young…

Love is the eye that sees beauty. In that one virtue there is light, and strength. There is daily food for the journey, courage and healing. We can add to this affection for our world a basic practice of meditation that quiets and clarifies the mind. Together, these two can enhance and deepen each other.

We struggle more than we need to, when we do everything but our inner work. That, we give short shrift. But this is that 'one needful thing'. With love, and regularly taking time for meditation and self cultivation, as a basis, and a way of life, we can begin to appreciate what Traditions offer, their great gift to us all.

In Tibetan Buddhism, basic ignorance manifests as what they call 'impure perception', or 'ordinary perception', the mundane view of the world that we carry with us, and this is seen as the root cause of how we limit ourselves and suffer. The opposite of this is called an enlightened view, pure perception, or sacred outlook. This is a way of experiencing the world as essentially divine in nature, having great beauty and potential.

The following principles go beyond Buddhism alone, to reflect something of what is seen and lived with in other Traditions as well, and in the lives of contemplatives. They stand in radical contrast and in eternal opposition to the common, mundane view. Here are few tenets of a magical world view, pure perception or sacred outlook:

that all life is sacred;

that the Divine, freedom and peace, the Kingdom of Heaven, is within us all

that our fundamental nature is pure

therefore, that we all have the potential to become free from suffering and attain happiness; we can accomplish great benefit for ourselves and others

that this world is sacred, alive and responsive, and that we are inseparably connected to it;

that we are always connected to each other, to our whole family

that there are other worlds, other realities

that there are many levels of beings, seen and unseen

that we are not alone in this world

that there are powers we can call on, Saints and Saviors, Buddhas and Bodhisattvas, Ancestors, and divine beings that will respond and help

that we are multi-dimensional beings, and so, things such as distant viewing, absent reading, and distant healing are possible

that there are faculties beyond the ordinary that can be developed, each according to our unique temperament and gifts, but to some extent by everyone

that prayer is effective

that ritual works

that mantra works

An enlightened world view, however we come to it, offers us spiritual food, expansive vistas, and the means to accomplish our aims; it offers us support, whenever and wherever it is needed most. I find such views closer to the truth of how things are. Whatever methods we then use, there is a workable operating basis for living that is full and rich. We are empowered by such views, and the heritage of our great resources is again, as ever, open to us.

From an enlightened perspective of this kind, the spiritual practices we do, such as study, meditation or prayer, aim to clear away what keeps us from knowing the truth about ourselves, and our lives here; the fullness of the gifts our teachers and benefactors have given to us, and what we have to draw from to act, to set things right as much as we can here in this world.

May we all be aware of our true heritage,
and live lives of generosity,

great joy, and fulfillment,
of great peace, well being,
and benefit to all!

Our Roots Go Deeper Than We Know –

A Reflection on the Power of Gratitude

In every traditional culture, we find parents and elders teaching their children gratitude, and the essence is always the same, that of cultivating a sense of appreciation for what we've received. Parents don't do this for their own sake, instead they do it as a gift to their children. They do it because they've known these blessings themselves, and know that this is what will sustain future generations.

When I compare how I feel when I have gratitude for my teachers, for my ancestors, and for the natural world, with those times when I lose this sense, there's a great difference. When I'm not aware of these gifts in any kind of tangible way, I feel impoverished, and living in a shadow that is the absence of joy.

I think many people feel this way sometimes, and what's more, what it means to have gratitude is not something that is talked about much in this culture, and so I thought to sketch out a few ideas about it here, for those who might like to pick up on this theme, and awaken more thankfulness in their lives. I marvel sometimes at the gift of friendship, and how it is a sustaining power in our lives. We may have only spent a short time with someone, years ago, but our time together was graced with a special quality that has stayed with us. Thinking again of that friendship brings that power to the fore. We are nourished by that love on a spiritual level, and it is this energy that gives us strength for all we would accomplish in the world.

We've received love, support and encouragement from our parents and teachers, and the quality of that love is something profound. Remembering that gift, we can't help but be moved, grateful, and dedicated to living a righteous life. Thinking of the lives of our parents and teachers, and spiritual ancestors, and of what they have offered us, we can see that they in turn were nourished by their own parents and teachers. This is what they received, and passed on to us, this love, encouragement, strength and wisdom.

When I say our roots go deeper than we know, I'm thinking of how we don't often look into the richness of what we have with us now. Generations have brought us to where we are now, and their sustaining power is here for us to know, and to be upheld and inspired by.

If we forget, we feel weak, easily intimidated by life. When we remember again who we are, and how we got here, we can't help but feel optimistic, and dedicated to caring for the needs of this time, and those of future generations.

To take just two examples of the vision and commitment that has come before, and that has brought us to where we are today, we can think of our modern education, and of the civil rights movement.

A century ago, ninety percent of the people in this country lived in rural areas. The recorded rate of literacy, even then was already high, but the level of education, compared to today was basic. During the last century, access to public libraries and to higher education has increased to the point that we almost take it for granted. Compared to a hundred years ago, many more of us have opened the treasury of learning.

It's only because people in previous generations saw the great value in public education that we have these advantages today, which are almost impossible to measure. All the knowledge of the arts, history, science and technology, and philosophy has come to us because of the efforts of generations of educators. Most of their names have been forgotten, but we have all this nourishment for our souls because of their love, vision and dedication.

When I look for examples of true heroes and spiritual ancestors in modern times, I can see that there were many great souls who only just recently came before us in the Civil Rights era. People who study that history know the names of Martin Luther King, Rosa Parks, Ralph Abernathy, Bob Moses, and A. Phillip Randolph. Looking further, we see that each of them were nourished and sustained not only by their fellow workers for human rights and dignity, but also by the labors of people like Ghandi, Emerson and Thoreau.

Every step the marchers were taking during those dangerous, difficult times was moved by love, and strengthened by those who went before them. They were encouraged to keep going towards justice, dignity and equality by those in their past, and by their hope for the future.

This same gift, this same power is what we've received, those of us who are heirs to their legacy. This is something that lives, something that we can touch again, when we remember them with gratitude for their great vision and efforts. And then, considering what we've received from them, how can we do anything other than try to take the next step to advance the cause of human rights in our own times?

It is this way too when we have the great fortune of connecting with a spiritual tradition. All those who have come before us, right down to our own teachers, have not left us. They have passed forward the gifts of their practice to us. Praise and gratitude awakens the sense that this really is so. Something of their power, kindness, compassion and commitment is with us now, and this is something we can celebrate and draw from every day.

Like a tree, through its roots, drawing up the sap of nutriments, breath by breath, we can reach down and feel our whole body fill with the health and strength, light, courage and love that is their gift to us.

We can remove ourselves from all these virtues when we hold the idea of ourselves as separate from all this – from each other, and from all our ancestors. This mistaken concept isn't something we would ever consciously plan to do – instead it's the character of a delusion – a result of miseducation, that persists, until it is unlearned, seen through and discarded.

There's a scene in the movie Amistad, where the character of John Adams is talking to an African man he is representing in an American court, and telling him how there's been a setback in the trial. At first the man, Sikey, doesn't understand, but then, when he does, he goes into a frenzy, and it's not until days later that Adams can talk with him again. When he does, he sees that Sikey is relaxed and smiling. He tells John Adams that he knows everything will be alright now. I remember he said,

'I spoke with my ancestors last night'
'I called them all into myself, and they assured me of our victory'
'I am the whole reason now that they lived'.

We can assuredly say the same thing about our spiritual ancestors – those who came before us and struggled to make this world a righteous place. The power of their work did not end with them, but is with us now. They had their work, the work of their time, which was not our work; and now we have our own work to do, in order to pass this same gift forward to our children, and the coming generations.

When you look at religions throughout different cultures and over time, you often see this gesture of looking back with admiration, and appreciation, with love and rejoicing at the gifts we've received. This brings it more clearly into the present, as a palpable force, as a revered energy and direction, by which we can live our lives. From gratitude, naturally comes works, effortlessly in a way, as the overflow of our heart of love.

I mark now as something really unfortunate when gratitude is glossed over, its depth and power as a practice and way of life not recognized. I think of jaded children and adults, having only superficial lives, with little joy to them. It doesn't have to be this way.

If we say we have counted our blessings, but then somehow remain unmoved, not uplifted and strengthened, then I know we've missed the vital point of gratitude. We've all received many gifts, by being here, and they are alive, and with us now.

May we all know the true measure of our heritage, to be living now, on this extraordinary earth; and *all* our noble ancestry, and with this energy, may we continue to work, in our own way, for the sake of our children, and our children's children.

A meditation on sufferings

Where many of the traditional teachings miss the mark for me is when they begin to talk about the sufferings of the lower realms. So often they talk about what I can't see, haven't seen, and it seems to be getting further away from a vital point, the longer they go on, and I listen.

This is not to say that what they describe is not true – for all I know it is true, and something to be feared and used to generate compassion. But I also have a storehouse of suffering images, and recollections that are far more powerful for me to reflect on – things I feel I can touch that have an unquestioned reality in this world of ours.

I've spent so much of this life looking at suffering that it's distanced me from any concept of a creator god I can believe in – omnipotent, compassionate;

it's also been what's brought me to religion, and kept me looking and finding what is of genuine use, with this reality of suffering as one pole to the search;

it's also been the cause of whatever moments of genuine compassion I have felt – the aim to remove the miseries of myself, my friends, family, people I meet, and those I think of from my meditation cell.

In a way, strangely enough, I count myself fortunate to remember what degradation is, what dense ignorance is, what the burning of restlessness, or desire, or the weight of depression feels like.

It's only when I gain some distance can these be thought of as anything other than a curse on being human. When there's a gap, and I'm not overcome with suffering, or despair, and I can see and feel and remember what I've been through, and think that many others are passing through these same experiences, and many more will go through them, then it steels my motivation to do whatever I can, with whatever resources I have or can find, to ease the way for them. I really know what is at stake.

To replace the sufferings I know with what is only imagined, as the teachings present it, seems like a loss of an opportunity to cultivate a vital and necessary quality, of determination, and connection with those who suffer.

The poetry may describe the harm experienced in other realms (or describe truths I don't see) but this world has more than enough for me to build up the feeling of a great wish to serve others as best I can.

I think of families grieving, like the one I saw in the waiting room at the hospital, for long hours. Two adult brothers, comforting their adult sister, who would from time to time break into tears – a parent was being operated on.

And I think of the loss of life on the streets, of people addicted to alcohol or meth, shunned by almost everyone, afraid almost all the time, living like an animal. The faces are etched in my mind, the smell, and the feeling of their hopelessness.

I think of the depression of a suicidal person. I've been that person. My family has been that person. My close friends have been that person.

I know two friends whose parents committed suicide. One was while I was in high school, and another I was told about a few years ago.

I think of divorced mother with a downs syndrome child. Or one with a child with cancer.

I think of a person like myself who's been in a number of relationships, and none of them has worked out.

I've spent most of my life alone, and have gotten used to it, more or less, by now, but this hurt is the very substance of my reflection on the pain of others, like myself.

I taste sweet fruit and watch as others dig through garbage, not looking up.

This world is full of misery. There is light too, and this adds to the tragedy of it – and gives an urgency to wanting to open the way for others to have more health and peace.

Our world, really, is an ocean of beauty, but it's not seen. Now, what to make of that?

We have the words - Economic exploitation – we not only don't want to think of this, we don't even want to really think of it, so we use language to cover it over. What does this really mean, that people live on so little each day? Who wants to look or feel what that is like? Who wants to think of what malnutrition means to a human life?

It's the same with human trafficking. We use words to cover worlds of pain.

We, most of us at least, are far too weak to really register the pain of this world. There are endless ways to escape or numb out, and, if I don't want to choose any of them, right there is where I need prayer.

Now, you may ask who I'm praying to, having said earlier that I can't conceive of a creator god - and it is an interesting question for me as well. I pray because I believe it matters to pray. I believe that there is an effect from it. If it hadn't have been for this, most of religion would have disappeared.

I have reason to believe, that can't be told, except to say I have had experiences of wisdom, compassion, presence and healing power that I only hoped and felt before might exist. These experiences, however few and far between, inexorably lead a person on, and so here I am.

I know that there are real, tangible spiritual potencies at work in this world, along with all the misery, tragedy, hopelessness and denigration of religious values.

I don't claim, by any means, to know the whole of it, but this much is enough to keep me going, and aspiring to know and facilitate the working of more of that in our world.

All the loss, fears, struggle, and pain exists alongside this truth, and so I try to bring them together. This much I can do. This much I will do.

From Regarding Tonglen

My friend Heidi asked

I wonder how we could find the right balance to get out of activity and stay in it at the same time, to increase our ability to spread the bright awareness in a kind of speaking silence. Any idea?

and I thought of how I can feel at times that we are so tangibly connected. I think this is where prayer is surely a way to continue sharing joy and strength. When we hold someone in our heart, we are never apart, and what we offer to one another is always available.

This is from Regarding Tonglen, in a collection of essays I have on Thought Training:

I've found the following simple and profound teaching, from the Western Esoteric Tradition, called 'moving up the planes', to be helpful: The idea is that we all exist simultaneously on different levels.

One application of this idea is that we may not have to be physically in touch with someone to be psychically or energetically connected; we do not need to be psychically connected to be mentally connected, or mentally connected to be spiritually connected, and to be a positive influence.

This kind of verifiable idea helps to cancel the mistaken notion we can have, especially when in meditation or on retreat, that it is somehow selfish to remove ourselves in some ways from others in need. Or the wrong idea that if we have removed ourself in some way we are not still connected on another, more subtle level. Sometimes, this is the best thing we can do, for all of our sake.

Westerners and Prayer

I thought to include this article here because it introduces the role of a world view. More is said on this subject in the essays that follow.

The practice of prayer comes naturally for many in the West, and the idea of serving others is there in us as well, powerfully. This is one of the reasons Tibetan Traditions have caught on as they have in this country. With their emphasis on compassion, sacrificing the ego and dedicating oneself to others, Americans find a match for what many of us already have in us, on account of our Western religious heritage.

Because of our often understandable estrangement from organized religion (read: Christianity) for many reasons, however, we've often been lacking the framework to think about, and the methods to put in to practice our noble religious motivations. Buddhism is providing these things for many people.

One thing that does seem odd to me though, these days, is how little Westerners who practice Buddhism know about our own religious heritage, and the many parallels that can be found.

It's ironic that Western Buddhists pray to Buddhas and Bodhisattvas, and to Buddhist saints for blessings, for protection, for inspiration and for healing, without seeing the parallels that Western Traditions have in them. Catholics, for example, have a rich tradition of praying to, or through, Saints. It's interesting that some feel at home making offerings and praying to the Buddhist Saints, without accessing sources that could be considered 'nearer at hand' so to speak. One day, I'm sure, Western Buddhists will include the person of Jesus, chief among Western Bodhisattvas, among the sources of blessings that can be invoked.

The West - Compared to Eastern Cultures

As Buddhist teachers are moving from the East to the West, it highlights some of the differences between our cultures. For one thing, modern Westerners don't have very much of a conception of other worlds besides the material. In contrast, Asian cultures' view of life includes other worlds, and other dimensions that influence their lives.

What we look at in Eastern Cultures and call 'Ancestor Worship' could perhaps better be called 'Honoring the Ancestors'. There are pictures of relatives on family altars, and many homes have a book with the names or their relatives going back generations. Every time someone is born, or someone passes away, and every time someone marries, it is entered in this record. Ancestors are honored, and their protection and wisdom is sought regularly (such as at the beginning of the Lunar New Year) and when there is some pressing need.

When I lived in Taiwan, one of the first things I noticed was that people were making public offerings, of chicken, fruit, rice crackers and incense, on tables set up in front of their homes and businesses, to what they call local spirits. Offerings are made with prayers for success in business, and for protection.

People in Taiwan frequently go to temple to make offerings and to pray for success or for guidance in business or relationships. I also sensed that a much higher percentage of people there consult fortune tellers. It's not considered as much as a 'fringe' activity - it is much more mainstream. And, in Taipei, there are many small temples dedicated to Buddhas, or Gods or Goddesses and Bodhisattvas or helping spirits that have specific purposes, for example to help get pregnant, or to pass an exam. There is a temple dedicated to Confucius that receives offerings around exam time. People photocopy student Ids and leave the copy with an offering at these temples.

In Asian cultures, people make offerings to appease ghosts, or spirits who would otherwise cause harm, especially during the time known as Ghost Month. Some people even conduct what are called Spirit Marriages to pacify the spirit of someone who died before getting married.

I say all this only to point out how culture is a whole way of looking at this world we live in, and the influences, for better and for worse that can effect our lives. In the East, the concept of other worlds influencing this one is woven throughout people's everyday lives. We don't have this idea nearly as much in the modern Western world view.

In Catholicism, people pray to, or through a vast array of Saints. They recognize the existence of Angels, and a Hierarchy of Spirits, and helpers, Jesus and Mary being foremost among them. In other centuries and other countries, people had more recourse to help from what we call the other side. Remarkably, in our modern Western culture we've lost this sense of other worlds and the beings and life forces that are available to assist us in our lives.

Prayer of all types calls on something greater than ourselves, or how we conceive of ourselves. It opens a channel between the worlds so that life and light can come through. Even if we are just saying, 'I pray I will be able to... stop smoking... to give up drinking... I pray I will have enough energy to accomplish this purpose...' we are referring to something greater, to some potential.

If it is true that we can tap in to powers beyond our usual abilities, and that we can transmit helpful, healing energies, then why would anyone choose *not* to pray? Perhaps overcoming disbelief happens slowly. In a materialistic society, Spirit and more subtle truths are denied, in many ways, from many directions, every day, until it is the dominant view that such things do not exist, and all other possibilities are temporarily shut out.

Here I can only encourage people to experiment honestly, as experience of spiritual truth is the only antidote to such harsh, anti-life materialism.

Some people say we don't need traditions, but it remains true that there is an abundance of resources available to us; energies, unique qualities to match our needs, and these have been preserved and transmitted and added to over generations in Traditions.

Reading the prayers from the various traditions, the essential expressions, both in terms of the ideas of the tradition and the energy of them, can help us to most quickly find what is suitable for us individually. This is vital for our own lives and the life of this world.

The purpose of Traditions is to benefit and to assist our reaching the Ultimate, the Source of all traditions, our true home, and living from there, and with that as a basis.

Oh, Good-hearted people! - I urge you to search out Traditions and methods to see what is effective for you - what riches there are for you, what powers that can help you and can help you to help others; what clarifies and can heal, and then share from this abundance that you find with others - with friends, family, strangers, with the whole world!

An Introduction to Buddhist Prayer

In America, and in the West in general these days, people don't usually associate Buddhism and prayer. We usually think of Buddhism as a tradition that teaches quiet sitting meditation, and it is certainly that. Right below the surface, however, we find that there is a great deal of prayer in Buddhism. Some schools, such as Zen, may seem to use prayer in the usual sense only sparingly, while others, such as the Tibetan tradition use a wide range of prayers for different purposes. There are prayers for healing, for cultivating compassion and other qualities; prayers to pacify difficulty, and prayers invoking the blessings of our teachers, Buddhas and Bodhisattvas, for support in all aspects of life.

To say what Buddhist prayer is, we would have to include two things: generally speaking, what Buddhism is, and, the nature of prayer.

First, as few words on the nature of prayer: What all prayer has in common, whether it is Buddhist prayer, or theistic prayer, is that prayer expresses a world view. Whether a person believes in God, or in angels, or in the intercession of Saints; or in the existence of Buddhas and Bodhisattvas, prayer shows what a person believes in.

Even more simply, with some people, praying shows their belief that prayer works for them, even if they don't understand completely why it works. We don't need to have a lot of philosophy behind it. If a person has some experience of prayer being effective for them, that is enough to get them to pray.

A universal human activity

It's clear that people worldwide pray for all kinds of things. It seems to be a completely universal human activity: for example, parents pray for their children, without having to be taught; people everywhere pray for good crops, and for safe journeys. I've heard one definition of prayer as 'a heart-wish'. In that sense, even atheists pray. And if there is a religious world view, then that is the form in which the prayer gets expressed.

As it is usually defined, prayer is reaching beyond what we usually think of as ourselves to receive support, grace and blessings from some benevolent power in the universe. It could be for ourselves, or for another, for a child or friend, or for the world. It is entirely natural, and spontaneous. It is the human expression of some need, or of gratitude.

Two kinds of prayer beyond words

In a brief overview of prayer, finally, there are two kinds of activity that need to be mentioned here, that are sometimes referred to as prayer, even though they don't follow the most known about pattern of using words. These two are silent prayer, and what can be called prayer-in-action.

The term silent prayer may be familiar to those who have studied Christian contemplation. Sometimes called 'the prayer of the heart', or 'practicing the presence of God', silent prayer can be a form or adoration, of thanksgiving, or it can be sitting quietly, with receptivity, a deep listening for guidance or for the answer to some problem.

A second type of prayer that may not usually be classified as such is sometimes called prayer-in-action. This is where it is not enough to wish for something, or to hope and pray for something with words alone, but when the opportunity arises, to sit still, or to speak, to recite, or to chant, or to move our limbs. This is inspired action, not separate from our prayers of aspiration. Here, there is a clear continuum between our thought and action. The same power flows through them, from the same original intention.

In both of these, silent prayer, and in prayer in action, there is experience on a level beyond words. Such prayer-fulness is then the state of a person's whole being, an expression of values, and an expression of their faith. Of course it will remain the case that most of what people identify as prayer uses words, but this dimension of prayer is also fully deserving of our recognition and respect. The deeper, more encompassing definitions will always be there, for anyone who wants to pick up on them.

The second part of introducing Buddhist prayer, after speaking of prayer in general, would have to be to say something about what Buddhism is. Buddhism is a way to live life with greater wisdom and compassion. Its teachings concern the nature of suffering, and propose a path that leads to the absolute end of suffering, and to genuine happiness. This is accomplished through meditation and insight into our nature.

Prayer comes into the picture as soon as we start to consider the role of cultivated thought and intention in the spiritual life. Buddhism teaches training the mind, and one of the ways we can do this is by learning to direct our thoughts in a positive direction, away from harming others, and towards actions that benefit. Prayers of aspiration can set our motivation for a session of meditation, for a day, or for our whole life. Examples of this might be for a person to pray, 'May I keep pure ethics today', or 'May I give up that habit'.

As with other kinds of prayer, the different kinds of Buddhist prayer express a set of values and a world view. Buddhist prayer, then, is prayer informed by a Buddhist world view. In every case, it is made up of a sense of where we are, and of the resources that are available to help; by what is going on and what is needed in the world and in the lives of living beings. It should be noted here that there is more than one valid, workable Buddhist world view.

A note on a Tradition that is beyond being theistic or non-theistic

In contrast to Western theistic prayer, Buddhism does not make use of the idea of a creator God. This is one significant difference. There are, however, many forms of Buddhism that recognize the existence of different levels of beings, such as devas, guardians, and local spirits. Many practitioners recognize and call upon the power and benevolent influence of our spiritual ancestors, present day teachers, as well as different levels of spiritually accomplished beings, the Buddhas and Bodhisattvas.

Lama Zopa Rinpoche has said,

'You are not alone, because all the time there are numberless buddhas and bodhisattvas surrounding you, loving you, guiding you, that is what they do..."

It may also come as a surprise to Westerners that, by sheer numbers, the great majority of people who refer to themselves as Buddhist practice what is called Pure Land Buddhism. Most of the Buddhists in Japan, Korea, and China, as well as many Tibetan Buddhists pray with great devotion to Amitabha Buddha, the Buddha of Infinite Light. Many millions of people recite his name-mantra 'Namo Amitabha' (homage to Amitabha) or 'Ami-tofu' and pray to be born after this life in his Pure Land of Sukhavati. This is regarded as being a heavenly realm, with ideal conditions for spiritual practice.

I think then that it's not enough to refer to Buddhism as merely non-theistic, and leave it at that. It is clearly not monotheistic, but it is, I would add, grounded in spiritual realities. Perhaps a better pairing then would be theistic and recognizing a diversity of spiritual life.

Generally speaking, theistic prayer is where you view the source of benefit as existing outside of oneself, and non-theistic prayer regards the sources of benefit as existing in oneself, or both outside and inside oneself. In Buddhism it's taught that ultimately the Buddhas and Bodhisattvas, and our own teachers are not separate from our own minds. Relatively, however, on the path we usually experience them that way, and so we can benefit from connecting with them and relating to them within that framework, as we develop a deeper realization of our own enlightened qualities.

One of the ways of relating to Buddhas and Bodhisattvas is as a method of cultivation, where the 'external' and the internal complement each other. Here, one meditates upon a Buddha form with devotion and prayer, as a way to identify and to produce these same qualities in ourselves. The forms are used to help us to awaken our own Buddha Nature.

It's often asked: does the deity (Buddha or Bodhisattva) have an external reality?, and answered, relatively, yes; ultimately, no (meaning that they are not separate from our fundamental nature).

The reason I would first begin by describing all Buddhist Prayer at this point as the expression of diverse people's world view is to try to be as inclusive as possible. The truth be told, looking at the range of what is taught and practiced as Buddhism, there is simply no one way. Some people relate to the world as having many dimensions, and many spiritually advanced beings, and others just to this one world that we more or less agree on. No matter. Many different cosmologies or world views can work when it comes to Buddhist practice, or to the activity of prayer. However our mind is, there is benefit to be found in prayer.

Take, for example, the wish, 'May you have happiness', or the verses for the cultivation of loving kindness and compassion, 'May all beings be happy', 'May all beings be free from suffering'. These are purely prayers of aspiration, and no faith is required in anything, beyond recognizing the power of love and compassion, and of our own thought and motivation.

From my own point of view, more important than the philosophy of prayer, is what all these practices point to. In whatever form we engage them they indicate the possibility of working with our heart and mind, and the possibility of transformation, benefiting ourselves and others. If we think prayer is something that could help us to accomplish this, there is plenty of room to have different world views and still have it work.

One example of a prayer that can work with different Buddhist world views, perhaps, would be recognizing that ethical action brings happiness, and unethical or hurtful action brings misery. We can then aspire or pray to live a moral life. Then, if our world view in addition includes the existence of Buddhas and Bodhisattvas, highly realized beings that live to serve others, freeing them from suffering and bringing them happiness, or a connection to teachers, then naturally we will ask for their help and support. 'May my teachers, and the Buddhas and Bodhisattvas help me to accomplish this.'

Another example of a Buddhist prayer and world view would be that elemental universal wish for our children or family to have happiness. If this is informed by an understanding of the causes of happiness as taught in Buddhism, ethics, the training of the mind or meditation, and wisdom, then that wish for them in that sense becomes a

Buddhist prayer. It reflects a Buddhist world view and understanding.

Again, if we include in our view the dimension of the existence of Buddhas and Bodhisattvas, and the blessing power of Saints and Sages, then, naturally, we reach to these sources of light and inspiration in our prayers, with the deep wish that they benefit those we pray for.

Here is a third example of what Buddhist prayer can be. By contrast, the peace of someone who has only known the effect that comes from taking a sleeping pill, and the peace of someone who has quieted the mind in meditation are very different. When a meditator or contemplative wishes for another to know peace and happiness, they have in their mind the inner peace and joy they have known. Such prayer is informed by their experience, the result of their Buddhist study and practice.

Buddhist prayer is the expression of what is felt by Buddhists to be ultimately worthwhile in life, and here is where another level of interest enters into it, if we want to know what many Buddhists are actually aiming to do when they pray.

All Buddhist prayer is informed by a Buddhist world view, on the nature of suffering and the path to happiness; of the preciousness of each life, and of our own potential. A fundamental prayer we can have from this perspective is 'May all beings have happiness, and the causes of happiness'.

Then, if we are practicing taking care of our own life in the Buddhist way, by cultivating ethics, meditation and the freedom that comes with wisdom in the Buddhist sense, one result of whatever liberation we achieve is naturally a greater dedication to all others. This arises naturally - it does not have to be imposed from the outside. This is how the path unfolds. Beyond the level of obscuration and affliction, our nature is compassion. From greater freedom, and greater empathy, our compassion can emerge. We can begin to recognize the fundamental equality of all, and to live our lives in response to that.

Enter the Maha-yana

What is called the Maha-yana, means the Great Way, in that, in its wish to benefit others, it aims to include all beings. A Mahayana Buddhist, in the best sense, sees that what we all need for our flourishing is something more than the material alone. What we need, ultimately, for our happiness and well being, is wisdom.

The Mahayana Buddhist Way of Life is in many ways the complete opposite of self centeredness, and of short sighted, hedonistic, materialistic culture. It is mature prayer. It is altruism. And although it includes ourself, it is living in response to the needs of the world and of all living beings. It is a willingness to give one's life to that task of freeing all others from suffering and to bringing them all genuine happiness. Such a motivation places us in harmony with life.

This perspective, of wanting to benefit all others, is more than a reflex, or a superficial emotional reaction. It is the result of contemplation, and an open hearted response, seeing our place in the world of struggling, suffering sentient beings. As Shantideva wrote: 'Although they long for happiness, they destroy the very causes of their happiness; and though they do not wish to suffer, they create the causes that bring suffering on themselves...' Such contemplations can shift the very center of our life.

Every Mahayana Buddhist, then, embraces what is called the Bodhisattva Vow as the highest ideal and aspiration, to free each and every sentient being from suffering and the causes of suffering, and to bring them all to immutable happiness.

We aim all of our maturation, our thoughts and actions, prayers and meditations to that objective, of benefiting all others in every way necessary, material and spiritual.

This Bodhisattva Vow, and bodhicitta – the thought Traditionally expressed as, 'May I become a Buddha in order to benefit all sentient beings', is a dependent arising. These causes and conditions come together: our perceiving the needs and seemingly endless sufferings of living beings, with compassion, and knowing a way out, naturally Vow arises from these.

Traditionally, as taught in the Tibetan Buddhism, before any practice, we set our motivation. We have the thought, 'May this be for the benefit of all…' and this is the great motivation that empowers the prayers and meditations of a Mahayanist.

After that, during the practice itself, whatever it is, we aim to keep a clear continuity of intention. And at the conclusion we dedicate the merit, the positive energy of our practice, to fulfilling our purpose, for example, 'By this practice, may all beings enjoy happiness, and the causes of happiness…'

When it comes to the activity of prayer, then, we can view Buddhist Prayer in terms of *path*, which is the cultivation of some motivation or quality, and in terms of *fruit*, which is what we give as a result of our practice.

Prayer as *a path* can be training the mind in ethics, or in loving kindness. We can reflect and cultivate the feeling, for example: 'Meeting this person tomorrow, may I have patience, and not get angry with them. May I develop the qualities that will help them as much as I can.' In some places, this is called prospective memory. As Matthieu Ricard taught, doing such meditations ahead of time that cultivate a positive quality, 'prime' us, or prepare us to engage with others in a better way.

Some people may wonder if prayer takes the place of meditation that calms the mind and by developing wisdom frees us from afflictions – meditation that has for millennia been regarded as the very heart of Buddhist practice. But it isn't the case that prayer replaces meditation, rather, at it their best, the practices of prayer and meditation are complementary to each other. With prayer we direct our mind and energy, and with calm meditation that liberates we can connect with and uncover more of our resources. We are able to offer something deeper and more useful.

In its broadest sense, prayer can be considered to be another name for Buddha Activity.

Buddhist Prayer *as fruit* then can be offering our light, and our peace to the world. This, at its best, can be a whole way of life for a Mahayana Buddhist. A Bodhisattva delights in benefiting others, seeing this as the most meaningful use of our life. No matter how difficult it is, no matter how long it takes, no matter what the cost.

The scope of this work is expressed in The King of Prayers, which has a verse that reads:

Limitless is the extent of space
Limitless is the number of sentient beings
And limitless are the karma and delusion of beings
Such are the limits of my aspirations.

And by Shantideva, who has the prayer:

For as long as space endures
and for as long as living beings remain,
until then, may I too abide,
to dispel the misery of the world

The Lam Rim Dedication has this verse:

With my heart going out with great compassion
In whatever direction the most precious teachings

have not yet spread,
or once spread have declined,
May I expose this treasure of happiness and aid

Cultivating this path, we become more able to intrepidly engage and to guide others.

In nearly every school of Buddhism, understanding the mind has a central place. The power of thought, and in particular the power of intention is expressed in the line by Lama Zopa Rinpoche, that: *'All of existence depends on the tip of a wish'.* Thought is the power we use to shape our lives. 'The tip of a wish' here refers to our motivation. One teaching says if the root of a tree is healing, the branches, leaves, flowers and fruit will all be healing. Again, it is brought out that our motivation is the deciding factor in the quality of our work, our spiritual practice, and in what we give to the world.

As with meditation and mantra practice, an individual's prayer can become a cultivated power. We don't know what we are capable of, and what effect our own meditation and prayer can have until we make an effort.

It's also true that the Traditional prayers we have received can be a great aid to our lives. Prayers that have been recited by many people for generations, with concentration and devotion, have built up tremendous power over time, and if we can connect with them, they can help us a great deal.

Add to this the fact that many of the Traditional prayers were written by people who are regarded as saints, such as Shantideva, Atisha, Tang Tong Gyalpo, and Tsong Khapa, as well as modern teachers such as Thich Nhat Hanh, Dudjom Rinpoche and Lama Zopa Rinpoche. As such, they are rich with insight, and blessings. Together with our own practice of having a good heart, meditation and prayer, we can gain the greatest benefit from Traditional prayers.

For some, to be a self defined 'person of prayer' can be a complete way of life, responsive and awake. Prayer can connect us to the Divine. It affirms our connection with each other. It can engage our creativity in the moment, connect us to Traditions, and help us to meet both suffering and joy. Prayer gives us a means to respond, and to offer, if not an immediate solution to problems, then at least solace, and hope, and the best we can give at this time, not turning away in spirit.

Seeing for ourselves the great value and effectiveness of prayer, who would not want to engage its practice in some form? It is completely natural to want to do so, especially when we see more and more of the needs that exist, and what can be done with prayer. We can direct our mind to virtue, link up with and draw from sources of great benefit, and share that with all. May all beings benefit.

The Prayers of Contemplatives

The prayers of contemplatives are not like ordinary people's usual prayers. In Buddhist language we could say they are spoken from the Dharmakaya of Ultimate Goodness. They have that vision, and that power and quality. As the poet Robert Bly said of images and verses that are spoken from a very deep level, they are charged, they are 'soaked with psychic substance'.

Ordinary people like myself, on rare occasions, can have some insight or inspiration flash to the surface, and, if we are smart, we hurry to write them down. A trained contemplative, on the other hand, has much easier access to the deeper levels of our true human nature, and less obstructing its expression.

We ordinary folks are very much a mixed bag – some jewels, and a lot of plain matter. But those men and women we call sages are pure channels – by their very nature, they are a stream of pure truth and blessings to the world.

Reading the prayers of contemplatives, we are nourished by what they give, and not only that. As important, we are also put in touch with that same profound level that they speak from - in ourself. To say that anything else is going on would be to put ourselves down, and to deny our own depth.

If we are inspired to read and reflect on the words of the Saints, it's because of the benefit that comes through to us from their level of experience. They are showing us who we are, what we have each received, and the gifts we have now to give. If we are inspired to think, or speak, or write our own prayers, this can also be something truly significant, a sacred moment for us. Our heart is moved, and it is actually light breaking through to the surface of our lives, and going where it is needed most.

The value in a contemplative's prayers, in the prayers of Traditions that have gathered power over time, is this same value that we can find in our own prayers today. It is made of generosity, and insight, and the delight of something reaching us, and awakening in us.

Each generation has its poets, its seers, it lineage holders, its light bearers. So who is to say who has 'got the goods' so to speak? From an individual's point of view, if their own prayer works for them, if it gets them 'unstuck', or brings healing energy, for me, that is proof enough. Whether it would work for someone else is another matter. Of so many things I am not sure, I am far from complete in knowledge. But what I am sure of, at this point in my life, is this:

1. that it's a great thing to read contemplatives' prayers, as great benefit can come from it

2. that it's a great good also to be inspired by them, and to think, and speak and write our own prayers,
and

3. that we should do all we can to encourage each other to pray as much as possible, or to put it another way – to access the deep levels of our true wisdom nature and to think, speak and act in the world from there.

Because of the great benefit that can come from it for us all, we should do all we can to pray our own prayers and the prayers of the Saints and Tradition. We should do all we can to fill the world with beautiful prayers.

The world needs our prayer, so much now, and what prayer can be at its best: the expression of our pure positive intentions, made of love and wisdom; vision, light, healing energy, nourishment, inspiration, comfort and joy. Prayer can illuminate, and can set our lives and our world in order.

However it moves in us, prayer is the quintessential human expression. It is our thirst for light, and the powerful deeply rooted-wish that we have, to give, in words and actions, of what we have found. Beyond disillusion, we find the way again through what I call prayer. I mean this in a way that is not restricted by any one concept of the Divine. It is open to every possibility, to every way of ever saying it.

The way opens again because of the heart's intent. The world opens, and the way forward once more becomes clear. May it be this way for us all.

Praise and Thanksgiving

Praise and thanksgiving are a part of every spiritual tradition for a very good reason - they help us to touch the deepest truths of our being here. We all need to connect with something greater than ourselves, that upholds and sustains us. Especially in times of difficulty, we need to look up:

"My eyes turn to the hills,
where I have received my help..."

Without this, our view is too small, and we don't know the resources of grace and blessings that have carried us this far, are with us now, and will continue to be with us for all time.

When we praise a brother or sister, a child, or a great and noble teacher, or what is divine in this life, in a way, we return their gift multiplied to them, and help their light to grow even more. Recollecting what it feels like to have the good in us encouraged, and how vital that is to our flourishing, we will then be sure to go out looking for opportunities to praise and encourage others.

Isn't the sky beautiful today?

Aren't the works of our brothers and sisters in this world a wonder to behold?

If we start here, every other kind of spiritual work, of contemplation, meditation, prayer and mantra all have energy behind them that they wouldn't otherwise have.

If we can stand back with some objectivity and take the time to appreciate our own work as well, it makes for a feeling of worth and belonging that is not so easily swayed by changing conditions, common values, or other people's opinions.

Praise all the good work going on in the world today, all the kindness, all the great far reaching positive motivations that our kin have; all the inventiveness, all the generosity, all the forgiveness, all the genius... it's all here, and our praise helps us to see it, and to be empowered by it.

From 'Lineage'

Namo Tassa Bhagavato Arahato Samma Sambuddasa

Homage to the Blessed One, the Noble, the Perfectly Enlightened One

"Lineage is very important in Buddhism. Lineage is not only the historical record and genealogy of masters who have held a particular teaching, nor is it only the teaching itself expressed verbally or on a page. These are important, of course, but what is even more important is the spiritual vitality of that teaching as it is transmitted from mind to mind and heart to heart. In other words, the lineage lives in the thoughts, words, and deeds of persons who have received, cherished, practiced, and accomplished it." - Khenpo Palden Sherab Rinpoche

When I remember something of what we are all heirs to, a new power enters my limbs, and I'm aflush with love and devotion. I am carried along, even as I labor. And how is *that*, exactly? Even I wonder at it, but if you want to know just what result can come from fellowship, and knowing yourself to be part of this family, this lineage, and the inspiration that brings, then I can only advise this: stay here a while, and then look at what is born. Surely we do our ancestors and teachers proud, continuing what they have given us, aiming always to do it justice, and adding ourself to it, as they would have wanted. This love now continues with us, fashioning the best of all gifts for those we meet, and for our children, and our children's children.

Blessings, Faith, and Devotion

The blessings of the Divine, of the Buddhas and Bodhisattvas, Saints, and liberated Sages encircle the globe at all times. Whether or not we are receptive to them, however, or draw these currents to ourselves, depends on our own inner state. This is where faith and devotion come in.

One kind of faith is receptivity. With it, we are open to something greater than ourselves reaching our lives, healing, illuminating, and guiding us.

Disbelief or spiritual pride block the receptivity we could have. Once we've made up our minds that things are a certain way, and that we are without support from the subtle realms, we've removed ourselves from the benevolence that is always here, at least consciously; And whether or not we put it in words, if we hold ourselves as equal to, or better than our wise spiritual guides, ancestors and teachers, we place ourselves above them, and can't receive very much from them. Humility is a prerequisite for learning anything, and never is this more true than when it comes to connecting with the divine in human form, or from the unseen, archetypal levels.

Alone one night, out of distress and shorn of pride, crying out, the hook of our faith can, in that moment, catch a pure force at work everywhere in the world. And our lives can change just like that. We may fluctuate, or even fall away from practice altogether for a time, but a seed of transformation has been planted. The world can become luminous again, larger by an untold measure, as new possibilities dawn.

Once faith has opened the way, and an intimation of a greater love and wisdom has reached us personally, the devotion that is then born is best described as a depth of love and trust that acts as a magnet for blessings. We begin to orient our lives around the sense of the divine wisdom that speaks to us in our own innermost language.

Faith then matures in us to a deep peace that comes from being held in tender, divine care, and from knowing our capacity to grow and change. Such trust in our teacher is also responsive. It strives to be ever more awake, learning the language of the heart that is becoming more sensitive to being guided.

The path develops in this way. We are not alone in our reaching for happiness. On the contrary, this world abounds with grace and blessings. If we are receptive to it, we can know this for ourselves, manifesting beautifully in our lives.

Saints East and West

{A brief essay on Saints, outlining their nature and activity, written as an introduction to the prayers of the Buddhist Mahasiddha Tang Tong Gyalpo.}

"Man generally is not conscious of the power he has. When a man becomes conscious of that power, he is able to do things which people cannot ordinarily accomplish." - Hazarat Inayat Khan

The mention of saints from the outset challenges our ordinary ideas of the way things are. The thought of extraordinary individuals has the power to shift what we conceive of as possible in this human realm. It also changes what we think of our teachers, ourselves, and our brothers and sisters.

A saint, both in the East and in Western traditions, is something more than a good person, or someone of exemplary character. Moving past this mundane conception, we enter into a supernatural framework for understanding the lives and influence of a saintly person.

In Western Traditions, and Catholicism in particular, we find a saint defined as someone who facilitates a connection with the Divine. They are formally recognized by the Church because they have been a factor in a miracle of some kind. Informally however there are many more people who are prayed to in times of trouble who are 'under the radar' of the official church.

The most frequently prayed Western mantra is the rosary, or the prayer to Mary, and a great many people over the centuries have reported experiencing her blessings.

In Judaism and Islam as well, the existence of holy men and women has been a part of their traditions of prayer and a source spiritual support.

When I was in Taiwan, I noticed that there were altars in various neighborhoods, where people prayed and left offerings. I asked the people at the school where I was working who as being prayed to there. They told me they were 'local gods'. I asked, How many local gods are there in Taipei? and, after going back and forth in Mandarin for a couple of minutes, my co-worker turned to me and said, "Fourteen". I later learned that in Taiwan' s blend of Buddhist and Taoist traditions, a person could, through their conduct and activity, ascend to the level where they are recognized and honored as divine. Quite different from our ordinary ideas!

As a Buddhist in the West these days, not much is said about saints, or holy people, or the help they can give a person. It's considered for the most part to be fantasy, or belonging to the realm of the mythological, at a remove from our actual lives in the world. And yet, the entirety of Vajrayana Buddhism as it is practiced today worldwide rests on this view that there divine beings or energies within and around us, that can be called upon, and that can help us in all kinds of ways. The well known practice of the Bodhisattva-Divinity Tara, for example, for many people has the reputation for being swift to respond, and for helping people in distress or in various forms of material or spiritual need.

In addition, some South East Buddhist schools as well have elements that can be considered magical in their working, although these are not nearly as well known about or discussed here in the West. In Thailand, in the last century in particular, there has been a subset of a tradition of monks making amulets for people's protection, and a legacy of stories of their effectiveness.

When we speak of a siddhi in Buddhism, there are two types, the ordinary, and supreme accomplishment. Ordinary siddhis could be such things as clairvoyance, a lesser or greater ability to heal, to pacify or purify a troubled environment, to control the weather, or to gather needed resources, The Supreme Siddhi, it's taught, is enlightenment, which includes all the other capacities.

Mahasiddhas, or Great Beings in Buddhism are those individuals, such as Tang Tong Gyalpo, who have extraordinary qualities and abilities to benefit others. Their words as we have received them have power, and time and distance are not obstacles to our receiving their positive influence. We may not believe any of this, of course, until we have some experience of it ourselves, and then even then, we may have some difficulty getting our heads around it. This is only on account of the persistence and strength of our habitual mundane views, on personal and collective levels.

There have been societies in the past, and there are still a few today that honor what is called Pure Perception, or Sacred Outlook. They are not easy to find, or receive with respect, but they do exist, for those willing to make an effort to find them.

In my own experience, I have the remarkable example of my own teachers, and witnessing the effect they've had on my life. I count among them even teachers I haven't met in person, but who for some karmic reason, I have a connection. And this is what it comes down to here, it seems, when talking about the influence of holy people, and spiritual beings of all types, angels, and ancestors. When we have a connection to one or more of them, it broadens what we think of as life in this world. We know we are not alone, and, what's more, in times of trouble we have a resource we can call on.

Dogmas often enter into into because of our differences, but it need not be that way. If we can see our connections with the divine as a personal matter, and our commonality with the others who make up our community, it opens the way to having respect beyond those names and forms and practices that work well for us.

Those great beings who have made their way onto our personal altar, or refuge tree are there for a reason. We have faith that is based on some experience of their beautiful effect in our lives, and in this world. It matters not a whit if others don't have the same experience. The spiritual life in this way is like eating. No one can do it for you, and no one can deny or debate your experience of being nourished and sustained spiritually. And so I offer this prayer:

May we all find strength and support throughout all our lives
May we share abundantly the riches we have received
from our teachers and from traditions,
and from the divine in all its forms in our life
and may there be peace and harmony, well being,
and an abundance of blessings everywhere.

The Nature of An Awakened Person

The *very nature* of an awakened person is to benefit others. His or her tangible qualities are like the sun; they are bright, and joyful, and endlessly beneficial to others. They are effortless, spontaneous, impartial, enduring, bringing harmony, joy and peace, healing, strength and encouragement.

I think of Thich Nhat Hanh, the 16th Karmapa, Lama Yeshe, Bokar Rinpoche, Tsultrik Rinpoche, Jamyang Khyentse Chokyi Lodro, Khenpo Palden Sherab Rinpoche, and Saints of other traditions, as having wisdom, as being free, and as effortlessly manifesting such virtues as these.

By their very nature, seeing them, looking at their photograph, or thinking of them now immediately brings light to the mind, and can re-establish health and harmony in a person. They are such powerful objects of refuge, faith and devotion for this reason. They bring peace and joy, and help us to awaken.

The perfectly divine, original nature that is known by and then is revealed in a Noble person communicates with words, by look, gesture, touch, and by its presence. This nature is what relieves suffering and brings happiness, everywhere and at all times. This light removes the darkness from the minds of ourselves and others, and destroys wrong views. It establishes people in right views about themselves, and others, and this world.

With buddhahood, or someone with any degree of realization, it's not that one achieves something and then just sits there peacefully, doing nothing. In fact, they are *most* active, for that is their very nature. In a saintly person, or in a Buddha or a perfectly awakened one, it can be most clearly seen how being *is* doing.

Even with an ordinary person, with ordinary states of mind, being is doing- their qualities are being manifested in what they think, say and do. We don't usually notice this however, since its not so pronounced. With a saintly person, an arahat or bodhisattva, it is far more tangible.

Buddhahood, the highest achievement of the contemplative life, the pinnacle, that which is most worthy of reverence, and the well-justified aim for all who would bring the greatest benefit to the world, is also the clearest expression of the divine life working in the world. This Buddhahood is *synonymous* with Buddha-Activity: It is spontaneous, impartial, intelligent, creative, adaptive, compassionate, and joyful, all without any effort at all. An awakened person is never separated from and are never unaware of their boundless, peaceful and free nature, therefore they can most effectively help others, while maintaining their view, and access to rich inner resources.

Prayer as Buddha Activity

Prayer is Buddha Activity - the awakened heart responding to the needs of the world. To think of it this way is different from the usual idea about prayer, but doing so helps us to understand both the act of prayer, and what is meant by a Buddha, or one who is Awake.

The mere gesture of placing the palms together may or may not be one of prayer. It all depends on what is going on inside a person. Someone can be thinking of anything at all. When they are thinking of and appealing to the divine, in the unique way that only they can know, then the outward gesture of prayer, in the traditional sense, matches what is going on inside.

Prayer has been described sometimes as a conversation, and at other times as praise, or as a deep listening for 'the still, small voice'. It can be an upwelling, an exuberance. At other times, and it can be an attending to what we know, buried deep within us, as a source of solace, guidance and encouragement.

Prayer has been described as changing *us*, and not the nature of the one prayed to. We become more receptive, more malleable, more attuned to truth and love. This is true whether our prayer is in the Christian context, to God, or Jesus, or to the Saints of that tradition, or in a Buddhist framework, to the divine as found there.

Rumi said:

Work on your stony qualities and become resplendent like the ruby

Prayer also reaches out, in every tradition, it moves through us, and into the world. This is true whether we are in our cell, meditating on the world as it is, and on the needs of our loved ones, strangers, friends, co-workers and adversaries of the moment, or whether we are out and about in our daily lives, speaking, and working.

I remember a book of Christian prayer I came across in India in the 90's with the title 'Prayer in Action'. Its theme was that there are forms of prayer that are active, and that are without words at times, doing one's share of the will of the Father, building the Kingdom of Heaven on Earth. This broadens the definition of prayer to divine activity, or to the activity of the divine in us and through us.

Dig a well in the earth of this body,
or even before the well is dug
let God draw the water up.

There is an effort to be made, then effortless-ness, something greater than our usual idea of ourselves becoming active.

There are the same ideas in Buddhism, and knowing about them helps clarify the nature of an awakened person, in any tradition.

There is an effort to be made, and then, when there is realization, or an awakening, the very nature of such a person is active. Whether they show peace and stability - I'm thinking of Thich Nhat Hanh and Ajaan Chah, sitting with such great stability and dignity- or whether they demonstrate the joy of the Way and the realized life, and thereby energize and encourage us, as with Lama Yeshe and Lama Zopa Rinpoche, and some Zen masters, their being *is* their doing. What they are, and what they have realized inside communicates and inspires, it edifies and uplifts the mind and the heart. It is like the proverbial 'stream clearing jewel', cleaning the muck from our thought and perceptions, revealing the beauty and preciousness of this life and the world.

This buddha nature - this original nature- also acts by organizing, by teaching, by writing and speaking, by giving food and clothing, and medicine and care, every needful thing. It heals. It is grounded in this present reality, and is far seeing. There is so much to be done in this world as it is now, but I have faith that we can awaken to the truth of our being here, and it is with this wisdom and compassion, this divine life, that we will continue creating a world based on truth, and love.

The Power of the Word – A Justification

The value of reading out loud, and recording, and listening to useful teachings comes from their being expressions of the truth. It does not depend on their being read with a mellifluous voice, or on the translation. Something deeper is at work, which I call the esoteric power of the word.

One part of Aryasura's Aspirational Prayer in 70 Stanzas says,

May all these beings be tamed
by relying on the sphere of action of my speech...

and he is referring to something more than mere eloquence, or to a pleasing or authoritative sounding voice. That *activity* of his speech refers to the function of the truth that is in his mind. This is something mysterious and profound, communicating mind to mind, where time is not a barrier, or distance; and where race, culture, language, and social status are all transcended.

Christians have long knows of this hidden aspect of the word, or idea, how it communicates power and blessing, and how it can inspire and guide us beyond what is specifically said. Through reading or listening, to be in touch with the Word is to be in touch with the Author of the Word, and in the case of a holy book, or teaching, it is to be put in touch with Truth Itself.

The Power of Truth in Buddhism also has a long honored tradition. Several early prayers recount teachings of the Buddha, and then conclude to the effect of, "because of the truth of these words, may our noble aspirations be fulfilled".

A recent commentator to this tradition, Piyadassi Thera, described the process of recalling the teachings as having the purpose of uplifting the mind of the listeners, even temporarily, to that level, where there is natural grace in abundance.

When it comes to spiritual subjects, a reading doesn't get its worth then from production values, or from classically appealing voices, or from scholarly translations. The value flows *through* these forms, to reach and to nurture generations of hearers.

The Resonance of the Saints

Even though a holy man or woman may have laid down their earthly form, their influence remains as a blessing to all who know them. This is hard or impossible to believe for the average materialist, and even in some circles where spiritual or religious matters are discussed, many have trouble accepting this idea.

In modern life, our senses are turned outwards. We may have grown numb and jaded, and disillusioned with false promises. We seldom register the slight changes that happen as a result of a written word, or an image; a voice, a melody, a color, or movement in the world. Still, if we were to train our attention to pick up on the usually small changes, they may lead us to discover marvelous things about our being here, and our connections to one another.

Usually when we think of some miracle happening, we assume it would be a gigantic change, something so out of the ordinary that it startles us awake into a new level of awareness. We imagine that something like a levitation, or an object materializing, or some illness suddenly vanishing without a trace would convince us we live in a miraculous world, however, it doesn't usually happen that way. There are great and small miracles happening, and we remain unconvinced.

I try to remember a line I thought of a few years back: 'The problem with a miracle on Monday is that by Tuesday we've forgotten about it.' Coarse and jaded we are, oh yes indeed.

The problem is that those dramatic moments so easily fade into memory, and disbelief. It would seem we would need to witness ever new and more impressive miracles to keep our faith going, and even then, I doubt we'd believe.

There is a tradition established in the time of the Buddha of not displaying any powers that were developed through concentration, such as clairvoyance. The reason was plain. The Buddha wanted to teach people the way to freedom. We can only imagine how crowds would gather wanting to see some unusual event, and if some display was made, that's what they would remember. They would go home having learned nothing.

When we speak of a holy man or woman, or a divine being, what we are referring to is someone who has reached the truth to an exceptional degree. Saints of any tradition can be known by their spontaneously ethical and deeply loving nature. They often have an elevating quality to them as well - we may feel blissful for hours or even days after meeting one. Witness the response many people have had to the Dalai Lama, or to Lama Yeshe, Lama Zopa Rinpoche, or to Amma.

That a holy person's influence remains after their body returns to the elements brings another level to it altogether, however. It means that, wherever we are, if we have faith and some connection to that teacher, or seer, or prophet, we can be enriched, uplifted, healed, and guided by them. This is not unheard of in the Indian Tradition. They realize that a saint transcends the limitations of his or her form even while they are alive, and that their blessings remain ever fresh and vital.

Often the reason people go on pilgrimage is to connect with the energy of a saint or divinity. Although a their presence is not limited to any one place, owing to the conditions of our senses, for some people it is easier to connect with that energy on an etheric level in a place where a saint has physically been.

People's respect and devotion to a holy person, or a teacher or divinity can also help us to connect with them. Devotees can consecrate a place or an object. They can literally help to imbue it with a particular spiritual power. More than once, I have seen and experienced how people's devotion can open a channel between the worlds, so to speak, between these different levels of being. (A few cases where this has happened can be found in the section called Miracle Stories, beginning on page_)

Even just hearing someone speak of their teacher with great faith and devotion can open up access for us, for a time, and we can see and feel and receive something of what they are so moved and inspired by.

I have thought that we need to develop our language to talk about spiritual things, as ordinary words and concepts do not reach into the mystery, as Rumi says. They often have a way of excluding from our vision and senses those deeper sources of nourishment, strength and guidance.

When we speak of the resonance of the saints, it is their being that continues, and that communicates through their works, and through their students and devotees. At any time, we can pick up on the energy of a healer, a humble, wise scholar, a lesser or more well known protector and benefactor, or a great world teacher. Knowing this for ourselves comes as a supreme gift.

We are encouraged to avail ourselves as much as needed of the energy of the saints and the divine life, for our own sake, and for the sake of our family, community and world. The problem is only that we are distracted, that our senses are so covered over, and that we so strongly disbelieve anything out of the ordinary. But even some slight opening on our part, some remembrance, and all our faith can be vindicated, all of our faith-lessness destroyed. After connecting to a saint, our old habitual sense of the world begins to fade. Our lives are blessed, and they become that much more of a gift to others.

Ocean of Saints - Invoking the Divine Feminine

Anandamayima
Amma

Teresa of Avila
Teresa of Lisieux
Catherine of Sienna...

Tenzin Palmo
Jetsunma Kushok Chimay Luding
Mother Teresa

Yeshe Tsogyal
Mandarava
Saraswati

Indigenous Grandmothers,
Holy Women of prayer and action,

Mary
Kuan Yin
Tara

Divine Activity,
gracing our world,

All you holy women, pray for us!
May your blessings be upon us!

Ocean of Saints,
Holy Women of prayer and action,
May your blessings be upon us!

Om Tare Tuttare Ture Soha
Om Mani Peme Hung

A few words on Ocean of Saints

We need to enter into the realm of metaphor, comfortably, to begin to speak of things as they actually are. We can see the limitations of ordinary language, how it mistakenly places objects and experiences outside of each other, and then attempts to convey relationship via subject-verb-object constructions. Things are both more simple, and infinitely richer and more complex than this.

When Christian theologians asked how many angels could dance on the head of a pin, by some they were mocked, as if they were looking for an actual number. The ignorance and arrogance of their critics couldn't be more obvious.

In the Avatamsaka Sutra, as recounted by Thich Nhat Hanh, angels, saints, and bodhisattvas come to the pregnant mother of the Buddha-to-be, to ask if he is comfortable. She expresses astonishment that, although there are so many of these holy beings, to offer homage to the future Buddha, they all are able to enter into her quite easily.

Since all is a manifestation of mind, or our spiritual nature, as expressed in this text, and this is limitless, there is no problem. There is always plenty of room.

In this very moment, we are accompanied by the saints and holy beings, enriched by their lives and presence in our lives.

When we count, in a religious work, or in poetry, we are at the threshold of the mundane world, and the spiritual realm. Counting is something we do in our everyday life, and we have to get it right, by consensus, in order to function effectively; counting out change, giving directions, agreeing on when to meet, and telling time.

In the spiritual world, there is one, there is two, as in relationship, and then there are numbers that point beyond all counting. If we miss this cue, it's as if our pant leg were caught on the doorframe - we get no further.

Moving through because we've understood the significance of the metaphor, we can leave behind numbers and walk in the light of spiritual presence and truth.

The question then arises, if one single saint contains the fullness of spirit, why mention two, or more? Our ordinary senses still obscure the the intangible, the beyond-conception. Seeing the same vital principle expressed in a few different names and forms disabuses us of the tendency to hold onto a single expression, and miss the inner truth that is being revealed. Once we get to that, then the essence of all the saints and holy men and women is there.

It's this way, then: Having one form of devotion to focus on, a name and form, a practice, focuses our mind and brings through the blessings. Devotions are our cultivated receptivity, and honor to have with us.

The Treasures We Carry

In their studies of Native Americans, African Americans, and Jewish descendants of victims of the holocaust, scientists speak nowadays of trauma being passed on through our DNA, and this feels true to me. It also feels like, once again, science is late to the game, catching up only now with what contemplatives, poets and healers have long known. And while it's true that we have inherited from our family lines the memories of harms that have been done, great injustices, and devastation, we've also inherited great riches from them. I don't expect science to catch up with this part of our human experience any time soon, and so I will have to at least try to speak of this here.

If it's possible to inherit ancestral trauma, in ways that can now be measured, then it only makes sense that we have also inherited positive experiences, insights and abilities from the past. These are also something we don't have to do anything to create or manufacture - they are our true inheritance. I would go further though than identifying as our legacy only what we've received through our parents. I would say that all of humanity's injuries, insights and qualities are ours as well. This was the idea behind what Jung called the collective unconscious.

Why is it that we don't know these things? I would say that it's the volume and intensity of our experiences that often blocks this knowledge. We have abundant resources in us, but are we able to quiet down, and to access them?

Our past and present familial inheritance is closer to us than the more general collective, and this is where most of us can begin our meditations to access the strengths and qualities that we need now.

My father and his father, mother, and grandfather transmitted their strength and courage, their creativity and great love. When I can tap into this, there's a fresh stream of light and inspiration I can bring into my work and daily living. The same goes for my mother's side of the family. Though I only met one uncle of my mother's, their guiding influence and love are certainly now a part of my life.

We can also speak of inheriting the lineages of social activism that came before us, and that are with us now, empowering each generation. All this is with us now, if we choose to tap into it, and use it in our work.

Our spiritual traditions and teachers past and present too have an element to them that goes beyond any one era, enhancing, vivifying, illuminating, nourishing each generation of practitioners. If we have a connection, and faith, then without a doubt, their blessings pour down on us, and move through our lives in profound ways.

We have all this to draw from in our life and work.

Touch the Present, Heal the Past, Create the Future

"You might think that the present moment is not the past, is not the future—but as you continue to look deeply into the present moment, you see that the present moment contains the past, and contains the future. And touching the present moment, you're touching the past, you're touching the future. And you can even heal the past, and create the future, while you dwell firmly in the present moment." - Thich Nhat Hanh

Whether or not we think about it, the past is a part of who we are now. This is true whether we are speaking about our personal life, or the life and history of our people, or our country. The sum total of our past is what brought us to where we are today. We may not want to think of the past, or acknowledge it, but it is here, and it influences how we see the world, and how we treat each other.

In a sense, the past is fixed. We can't change what has happened. What is not fixed however is how we now understand and choose to carry the past going forward. In other words, the present is not fixed. We have choices, and so the future is not yet determined.

Some people either deny what has happened to themselves or in this country, or they give it scant attention. But this is simple math: if we want to come to terms with something significant in our own life or in our history, we have to give it the time it deserves to understand it, to reconcile ourselves to it, and to remedy and heal its effects going forward. If we don't give these things enough time and attention, choosing instead to move on in a facile way, at best we'll get a small result in terms of health and insight, in the times ahead.

Where is this past to be found? It is found in our very bodies. If we learn to steady the mind, focus in, and look, we can see that so many causes have come together for us to be here as we are today: magnificent causes, tragic causes, uncountable blessings, unspeakable sadness. Because we all have this natural wish for our own happiness, and that of our children, friends and neighbors, we need to look at what will secure the peace and well being that we seek. Our past, individually, as a people, and as a country needs to be looked into to see what got us here, and so that we can secure the best outcome, for ourselves and loved ones.

Sometimes we may avoid looking at the painful parts of our history because we feel we can't do anything about them. We may feel we are not up to the task of healing it. We think that to look would just be reopening old wounds, and we recognize that sometimes the best thing we can do is to leave things in the past. But there is a whole category of events that don't heal completely by leaving them alone, and *those* we need to understand more deeply. Moreover, *we need to recognize the capacity we all have to heal the past, in the present moment.*

Thich Nhat Hanh said something interesting a number of years ago when talking about the three times. He said, *Touch the present, heal the past.* Clearly, not all the ways of accessing our history has a healing effect, so what did he mean by this? *I think he was talking about touching the past with love, and with the intention to care fully for this body, and for the wounds we have carried so long in our heart, as our heritage.* If we are not to perpetuate the injury and anguish of what's come before, we need to bring our very best resources to bear on this body.

All the past suffering that has come down to us, and that has shaped us and influenced who we are now can be met with mindfulness, and compassion, leading to insight and healing. We don't need to be prisoners of the past. If we train ourselves, we can become free individuals, and pass that on as our gift to our friends, family and future generations.

Past, Present, and Future; Politics taken to the level of Spirit

We may think that we can leave some things in the past, socially or personally and that they will self-correct, or leave us in peace. There are some experiences that are like that, no doubt, but the really formative events don't go anywhere, even when the surface changes. They can be like roots pushing upwards beneath what is seen in our lives or in our culture, waiting for a chance to manifest. Not only does the past live on in us in some way, it can recur, and even take more terrible forms. It also conditions how we experience our lives now, acting as a filter, and shaping our values and responses to what we know. Not only is our own history included in this, the history of our family and ancestors is here with us as well.

Both our personal story and our history are an inheritance we carry, and both can be held and understood and healed in us, if we make this a conscious choice. We do need to step back from repeated injuries, and stop them from happening, and that is an important first step, but by itself this doesn't go far enough.

In the enlightenment story of the Buddha, during the first watch of the night, it's said that he remembered his past. Certainly it was a past that experienced many kinds of suffering and misunderstanding, but that then became the foundation for his wisdom.

Where do we find forgiveness, for ourselves for our own wrong actions, and for others, individuals and groups? I've noticed that for me, whenever forgiveness happens, there are causes behind it, principally those of understanding that it's confusion that leads people to harmful actions, and my own wish for peace. To be more precise, without an insight into *my own* ignorance and suffering, it's likely that I'll put myself down, and that I'll blame others and lash out at them. Being close to and understanding our own evolution out of bewilderment and misery opens the way to having compassion for others, for forgiveness, and healing, in ourselves and our world, going forward. This takes a lot of courage, and a great deal of faith in our potential to heal, and to become whole.

In the Buddha's teaching on loving kindness, he said that we should extend our care to those *already born, and yet to be born.* This is in complete accord with the First People's view that we should take care of each other and this earth in a way that reaches to the seventh generation. How to do this? How to live now? We must think deeply about these things, especially now when so much seems to threaten our survival.

In this very moment, in this very body
we practice looking deeply,
embracing our loved ones, and this earth
with all our care

We have inherited not only the errors and harms of the past, but also our ancestors' great wisdom, courage, and compassion. Look within - this is also what we carry with us now. These holy gifts have been passed down to us through the generations, to be drawn from especially in times like these. So many times when we want to change our culture we are facing outwards, racing all over, when we should be looking within at what we carry, and our potential. If as individuals we take the healing of our world in ourselves as far as we can go, this is the best thing we can do. We have to take this healing to the level of the spirit, both for our own sake, and for all of our loved ones.

The following is a poem I wrote about healing ourselves and our world, as we have received it, right here in this very body and mind:

All the ancient suffering,
of exclusion, and exile,
of discrimination, and persecution
All the wounded memory, held tight,
and fears -
oh, for there to be ease!

If this sorrow is not to continue
for generations to come,
what is sought,
the vision carried,
needs to be known *now*,
as a balm reaching back
all the way to the first injury,
and forward,
flourishing through the ages

We may have an idea of ourselves as separate from each other, from our natural environment, and even from our past and future generations. This deeply held idea keeps us from knowing ourselves and each other as we truly are. Once we've moved beyond identifying with an ego-idea, understood it as a mere convention and seen through it, the world opens up. Because we are connected in profound ways with our world and with each other in every moment, communication is possible.

Once you have demolished the world which is built on the foundation of ignorance, then wisdom itself moves to build a world based on the foundation of wisdom. - from an oral teaching by Tara Tulku, as told to Robert Thurman

In the Avatamsaka Sutra, a Buddhist teaching from the first century A.D., there is an image called the Jeweled Net of Indra that describes how we exist in the world, and how the world exists in us. It is imagined as a net as vast as the universe, and on every intersection of the net is a jewel. All the jewels are reflected in each one jewel, and each one is reflected in all the others. We exist in this world right now, and the totality of this world exists in us.

We are not closed systems. Because in this very moment our bodies and minds are permeable, porous, we can breathe, receive oxygen, eat and digest food, and listen to and share knowledge and information with each other through time and space. Communication is possible . How then should we live? How can we best care for ourselves and each other? One of the secrets of this mind of ours is that it is not only an organ of perception, it is also an instrument of transmission. We can receive and transmit blessings and healing energy with our mind. We can heal ourselves, and help to heal our loved ones and our world.

Once we know our connection in this very moment to our world, to one another, to past and future generations, and our own potential, it changes how we view personal and collective problems. Let us then bring the very best qualities of mind to these challenges we have now, and those to come, and heal it all, down to the very roots. We can do this with great love and compassion, with meditation, and prayer, with mantra, ritual, and good works, and in all our relationships.

The following prayers are based on teachings by Thich Nhat Hanh

I carry the experience and wisdom of my ancestors,
and I ask them for their support, protection and strength...

and

I see my teachers and spiritual ancestors in me
and I open myself to their inspiring, positive energy...

*I vow to practice to transform the suffering in myself
and in all others,
and to transmit their love and wisdom to future generations…*

Great River of Compassion -
An Introduction to Mantra - for Westerners

Avalokiteshvara, help me to say this rightly, for all who could benefit from it.

Mantra:

I: A set of sacred syllables, repeated to attain a spiritual benefit

II. From the Sanskrit: A tool for thinking. 1. Prescribed syllables, in Sanskrit, to protect the mind from defilements. They express the essence of specific energies. The recitation of mantras is sometimes done with specific visualizations. 2. Often, Mantra is used as a synonym for Vajra, or Tantra, as in 'Mantrayana' - the path of mantra.

In thinking about writing this introduction, I've tried to bring to mind the most commonly asked questions about mantra practices. I know, first off, that most people have no interest in this subject, feeling completely sure, for some reason, that these practices don't work, and that it's a meaningless subject for them to learn anything about.

A second, much smaller group tend in the opposite direction - without trying things, they believe what they hear. They take it on faith, or because it sounds reasonable, or because it fits with their world view of what's possible.

Both of these extremes, of tending toward credulity, or a pre-judged disbelief, would have to be set aside, before anything new can be learned, especially when it comes to more recondite subjects - where there is a lot that is hidden, or subtle - outside the range of our usual perceptions.

Instead of believing or not believing from the outset, perhaps someone new to this subject could listen to these ideas more as an invitation, to try some of these practices, or to see things in a different way.

I hope in these pages to be able to share some basic information, and to offer as much as I can in the way of warm encouragement to practice. The effects can really be great, profound and life-altering. They can change what we think of as ourselves, and what we think of as 'a human being'. As Rumi said, "Human beings are mines..." We have all these richnesses inside us. All these potentials. May they manifest effortlessly in whatever way, and as much as necessary for the benefit of living beings.

Imagine if someone told you that you had a pot of gold right around the corner from where you are standing, in your very own backyard. Whether or not you knew this person, it would at least be worth a look. If they even said that you had a single gold coin, most of us would at least look. The usefulness of money is something we can all relate to - 'no harm in trying', we'd say. And yet, compared to the claims that are made about the power of mantra, the usefulness of money is limited, almost nothing. There are other kinds of wealth near at hand that we can have access to and make use of.

Our body contains medicine

When we're first introduced to the idea that there are healing properties within our body and mind, that can be contacted and increased, we might be surprised. After all, it goes against everything we've been taught about who we are - and these beliefs can be quite solid.

If someone says to you that your body contains healing properties that can be awakened and increased, it's like being told that there's gold nearby, in your own yard. First, you'd want to know where, and second, how much! Well, the teachings on mantra provide the 'where' - the directions, if you will, to inner treasures.

As far as the 'how much', I'll repeat what tradition teaches, and that is, that it depends on the person and the practice itself what will come about. As always, there is the invitation to practice, to experience and see for yourself, along with the encouragement that these practices could be of great benefit to yourself and others.

If you find you are interested, then please do give these practices a fair try, in terms of time and effort, as it's said, to awaken the energy of the mantra.

Working from two directions

Let's say you want to cultivate compassion. You may choose to recite the compassion mantra, OM MANI PEME HUM. An experience like this may follow: you can feel peaceful, and have a warm feeling. You may see light like sunlight, rising from within. You may want to share that feeling or express that feeling in some way…

While reciting, you may pause, and say, "may all beings be happy", "may all beings be peaceful…", or make prayers of that nature.

The feeling then can be somewhat different - as if you are using a different part of the mind to cultivate good-will, love and compassion.

Reciting the mantra, you can have the feeling arising from within, surfacing, as it were, from the depths. And then, praying, or thinking May all beings be happy, from a contemplative level of mind, deeper than ordinary thinking, you may feel this same feeling is both being cultivated or awakened by your prayer, and also changing your surface thought and feeling.

Two explanations for why mantra works at a deeper level

It's taught in both the Indian and Tibetan traditions that the sounds of the syllables of mantra themselves have power. They embody, or express, or are the quality that we aim to produce, experience, or cultivate. The sounds are themselves the quality we aim to experience, and to make use of to benefit self and others. This is one explanation.

The other explanation is that, through use over generations, mantras have been associated with qualities, or states of consciousness. And when we repeat the syllables of a mantra, we tap into a reservoir of particular life-energy, or power that has been built up over time.

Either way, if it works, that itself is proof enough. We really don't need a theory, though it may clarify some of what goes on. Personally, I feel there is truth in both explanations as to why mantra works.

Often when we read about the use of prayer or mantra, we read extraordinary statements - far from our usual world view. And I must say, in all honesty, that there is something in mantra that is beyond description, and that needs to be mentioned.

More food for thought - On world view

I recall reading early books about Tibetan Buddhism, the branch of Buddhism where mantra has flourished. They referred to the Tibetan Tradition as "Magical Buddhism", and in a way they were right. The starting point for much of the prayer, visualization and mantra in the Tibetan Tradition is what can be called a magical world view.

A magical world view, wherever it is found asserts levels of reality beyond the physical world, and that there can be interaction between the different levels

- in a magical world view, thought, or more particularly focused thought, is considered a creative force, a world changing force, to a much greater extent than is commonly believed.
- often in a magical world view, spirits of different types can be called on for assistance in various matters, and they will come – ancestors, saints, forms of divine beings, such as angels or bodhisattvas, or saviors
- sometimes in a magical world view, the whole world is thought to be alive, sentient
- Magic, in it's most general sense, is changing the outside world by changing something in the inside world. This is often accomplished by ritual, or by prayer, meditation, the use of mantra, or a combination of these.

Sometimes it's asked, with so many mantras, where should a person begin? I think of one analogy I heard years ago, that points to an answer, and that at the same time offers an explanation of why one mantra may be more suitable for a person, and another not work for them. It goes like this:

Imagine a field or a plot of land, and beneath the surface of the earth, at different depths, are different kinds of seeds. The seeds that are closest to the surface are those that will give results first, or the most quickly. This is why gurus, or teachers with insight into a student's nature, their 'field', so to speak, are traditionally the ones who tell the student what mantra to practice.

The theory of karma - past experiences determining one's character and affinities - can be useful for some people, but it's not essential to accept as a prerequisite for practice. Just do some practice and you will see for yourself what mantra brings you what, if any results.

The quantitative and qualitative aspects of mantra practice

When we make contact with a tradition through study, recitation, chanting or mantra, we can feel that we connect with a flow of energy to some extent. It may be a subtle feeling, or it can be something stronger, like a steady current. Sometimes it can be quite a forceful experience of energy, of a certain type of life that we are in touch with.

It can be like opening the sluice of a canal. We can feel we have contacted some source of energy, and we can feel it moving in us or through us. (See 'Imagine an underwater system of channels…' - the short poem on page_.)

However, if we only talk about a quantitative increase in energy, as if life-energy were just a generic force, like water or electricity, that would not be saying enough. It wouldn't fully describe what we meet with and utilize when we connect with a tradition or make use of a mantra. We also need to speak of the qualitative aspect of spirit.

Ajaan Lee said this about the worth, or the value and power of certain states:

"Things that are genuine, or pure, even though they may be small, can give rise to enormous results. Just as a piece of genuine paper money - a tiny strip of paper with the state seal - can be put to use in all sorts of ways. But if it's newsprint, even a bushel of it wouldn't be able to buy a thing. In the same way, a pure mind, even if we can make it pure for only a little while, can give rise to results way in excess of its size."

And, in speaking about specific qualities, here's how one teacher named Mingyur Rinpoche replied when asked, "What does blessing mean?"

He said, "It is a particular type of power…various medicines have various types of strength, or power. Water has a power to wet things and clean things. Fire has a power to burn. When we put water in a field, it helps to grow flowers or crops. All phenomena have a particular power associated with them... Blessing comes as a particular type of power." (to accomplish a specific purpose).

For example, when one prays, "Grant me your blessing that uncontrived devotion may arise in me", What happens is, that one receives that power, the blessing, and one's defilements and obscurations are purified and dispelled. If one gives rise to devotion and faith and supplicates, then one has the blessing connected with arising of faith and devotion."

Many different practices

There are many different mantras, and many different practices that one can choose. Sometimes these are called 'yidam' or 'deity' practices. It think it's important to consider clearly here what is meant by the word 'deity' in Buddhism. This is a difficult word for Westerners. We have a 2000 year monotheistic tradition that is in our Western soul, and any term that brings to mind our Western Tradition needs to be considered carefully.

All of the qualities represented by figures in Buddhism are within each of us. Every quality, of love, intelligence, purity, healing power - but usually we don't see ourselves this way.

If our self view were to fluctuate, even a little, we would find that simultaneously the way we view images representing enlightened qualities would change too.

If we see ourselves as ordinary beings, and we experience ourselves as fundamentally without these qualities, then naturally if we think of Buddha's or Bodhisattva's qualities existing at all, they are felt to exist outside of us.

If there is a change in our self-view, or the way we experience our self-nature, then when we look at these images we can feel that "this quality is there - it is in Tradition and it is in me, as potential perhaps, but in the same way the fully developed flower-and-fruit giving tree is in the seed and the first shoots".

In addition to their being an external, historical aspect, like a reservoir of a particular energy that can be contacted, we can also feel that the image or the idea of what is called 'a deity' represents aspects of our own nature, fully developed.

Perhaps when we are there, when we are the fully expression of some enlightened quality, then we could look at the image, sometimes called 'deity', and, with understanding, say "That is me".

There may be one place where the Western idea of a deity and the way it is made use of in the Vajrayana overlap, and that is in it's external aspect. Names and forms of Buddhas and bodhisattvas can be called on, and they will respond. Not for everyone, and not always, but this is an inherited truth, this has been many peoples experience in many places throughout time. I've had this experience myself on many occasions or else I probably wouldn't be writing this.

Actually, many people have had the experience that mantra and prayer really do work in the ways they are praised - to heal, to harmonize, to clarify. But, again, as we say 'the proof is in the pudding'.

My feeling is that if others, or if even one other person could hear about these things, be inspired to practice, and gain some of this benefit, then my efforts here will have met with success. So I know I at least have to try to speak of these things.

To call on a holy Name, and to feel some response, this is precious, of inconceivable worth. But there is more intended by the practice of mantra and the forms passed down to us to be meditated upon. We can receive their benefit as needed in our lives. And we are also encouraged to cultivate this understanding, that we all have all these qualities within us.

We are encouraged to bring them out as much as we can, and to live and act in this world, in enlightened and enlightening ways, with compassion and wisdom.

Mahayana

What's called 'Mahayana' in Buddhist traditions refers to a re-orientation towards teachings, self, and others in the world. All Buddhist lineages have teachings about love and compassion, but in Mahayana this aspect is placed right in the center. In this way of thought, the needs of all others, inclusively, and compassion for all is emphasized, and then every other practice, such as calm meditation, contemplation on mortality, karma or realizing selflessness, is seen in relation the suffering and confusion of living beings.

All these teachings then take on vast importance. When practiced, they can help us first to help ourselves, freeing, awakening, and increasing our ability to help, and they can directly help others. When held, and maintained, all these teachings and practices can be seen as being not just for ourselves. And then their potential, to bring happiness and to remove suffering, can be perceived to be as it is - as something enormous, limitless. Seen this way, our appreciation of the value of these teachings can increase enormously in our mind. These teachings and practices have the potential to benefit self and others. They can open the way to peace, health and every enjoyment, so their value is naturally very great.

What then to say about mantra? In this context, a Mahayanist, whether they think of themselves as Buddhist or not, someone who has bodhicitta heart, the intention to remove as much suffering as possible and to benefit others as much as possible, naturally will look in an unprejudiced way for whatever can help. Naturally, there will be no obstacle to that kind of determination to help. What joy, then, when someone with these pure, good intentions, finds the study and practice of mantra. Even if this is not for everyone, due to karma and people's affinities, still, who would not be intrigued?

In the true Buddhist spirit of free inquiry, the way is open, and the warmest invitation is given, to try the practice for oneself, to see if they work as described in many places, or possibly too in ways that are even better. Of course, they may not work at all, but for those with an affinity with any of these practices, the results for oneself and for others can be very great.

On Mantra and Initiation -

Often before beginning the practice of a mantra, a person will attend a ceremony called an initiation. This is helpful, to introduce a practice, and to further realization, but it is not essential to begin or to receive the benefits of a practice. If you begin some practice, and get some positive result, then you may like to consider attending an initiation. This can strengthen your practice, and facilitate realization. An experienced Lama can share his or her energy, and connect us to a living lineage of practice, and this can be something really profound.

Some people gladly travel great distances to attend initiations, because of how important they feel these events to be. If you have any interest, and the chance to attend an initiation, by all means do take the opportunity. You can check with your local Tibetan Buddhist centers for a schedule of events and initiations, which are also called empowerments. Usually there will be some teachings or commentary along with the ceremony that will explain what will take place and how to practice in detail. Until that time, however, mantras and practices are available.

It's traditionally taught that what's called 'self-generation' - where one visualizes oneself as the deity - should only be done by those who have received the initiation of a particular deity, but that 'front generation' - where one visualizes the deity in space above and in front of oneself - can be done by anyone.

In front generation, we visualize, or see with the mind's eye above us, the Buddha or bodhisattva whose practice we are doing, and whose mantra we are reciting. It's helpful when doing this recitation and visualization, to see pure light and nectar streaming from the image we hold, and that is also made entirely of pure light. These represent, or carry the blessings of the Buddha.

We should also see ourselves, our own body, not in an ordinary way, not as flesh and bone, but as also being made entirely of light. Many teachers advise, too, that when doing this visualization, we see ourselves in a pure land, and make the visualization as beautiful, peaceful, perfect, and pure as we can. This is helpful. We can also do the practice without any elaborate or detailed visualization. We can just see light above us while reciting. Or without any visualization at all, we can just recite the mantra.

People ask, 'But isn't this all just the imagination?' And the answer is... yes, and... no. It may begin that way, but sometimes something else, something quite wonderful, can enter into the practice. When done properly, by someone with an affinity for a particular practice, we can receive benefits far more than we could ever have merely imagined. We can tap into something larger than what we usually think of as ourselves, and receive fresh energy and inspiration. We can receive and awaken these different qualities that then can be made use of to benefit self and others.

May all beings be free from suffering
and the causes of suffering
and may I be the cause of this
May I contribute to their freedom from suffering
as much as I can

And,

May all beings have happiness and the causes of happiness
and may I be the cause of this
May I contribute to their happiness
as much as I can
May everyone receive, understand and practice well
the teachings that will benefit them the most,
freeing their minds from suffering and confusion,
and may all arrive at peace, fulfillment and joy in this very life.

An Introduction to the Bodhisattva-Divinity Tara

In order for us as Westerners to engage in practices that have come from the Tibetan Buddhist Tradition, without misunderstanding their nature or purpose, there are a few ideas that need to be spelled out. As Americans, we have certain common ideas, and so the same questions naturally arise, and these can be addressed at any point, but probably the earlier on in our study the better.

I would like to introduce Tara as an example of a practice that can be beneficial, and, when I think of doing this, I can see right away the kinds of questions I would propose we consider so the communication can have a better chance of success.

First, as with any divine being – or bodhisattva, we have the question, 'Who is Tara?' Of course we can see that there are different ways to answer this kind of a question. There are different levels to it. When we speak about the ultimate nature of anything, be it God, or Buddha, then this is a really deep question, maybe taking a lifetime to ask or to answer. If we are asking this type of deep question, this holds up a mirror to our own self. We can ask, 'Who am I?', and 'Who do I conceive myself to be?'

Then again, especially if we are beginners, we really need more of an answer in terms of what we can all easily recognize and understand and work with. Maybe this approach will be helpful: using the simplest, least esoteric language to describe something that is both accessible and also profound.

Historically, and now in Western culture too, Tara is regarded as a protectress, a savior, a benefactor. The practice of calling on Tara in times of need has been successful for many people. She is called on to help liberate us from problems, and especially from fears. She has a reputation for quick action, for responding very quickly, with loving kindness and compassion.

Her practice can be done in different ways - with prayer, or through visualization and mantra recitation. Tara's mantra is Om Tare Tuttare Ture Soha (pronounced Om Tah-ray Too-tah-ray Too-ray So-ha). A person can also simply think of her and feel her presence with faith and devotion.

Meditators will tell us that we all have Tara within us; that all these qualities and wonders are contained within our fundamental nature. They tell us that if we do the practice these qualities awaken and are expressed in the world, and that in a sense we become Tara, and this I don't doubt. For the time being though, let's just stay with the outer, common belief and function, that calling on Tara works, that increasing what we can call *the Tara energy* in our lives works, even if we don't know all of why or how it does. If we have some karmic affinity, and some receptivity or openness, and we give these methods a fair try, we can see the result for ourselves.

'If I could only give you the moon...'

Another question that often comes up when talking about any of the bodhisattva-deity practices, calling on Tara for example, and praying for a husband or a wife, or for health, or wealth is, 'How is this Buddhist?', and I think I'm just now able to say what I've been thinking and feeling for a while now that Tara is of a certain class I call 'the Bodhisattva Sangha'. The word bodhisattva means someone who is dedicated to helping others in the fullest possible ways, and sangha means a spiritual community.

As a member of the Bodhisattva Sangha, Tara responds as we would, with kindness, to someone asking for something... If they ask for water, we give them water; if they ask for a coat, we give them a coat...

There's a Zen story about a monk who was told that a thief was coming, and so he threw his bowl and his robes out the window as the thief approached. The thief scooped them up, somewhat startled, I'd imagine, and the monk called after him, saying, 'If I could only give you the moon!...'

Such is the wish of Bodhisattva Sangha – their deep wish is for our true happiness, our freedom, peace and health, and so if we ask for food or shelter or medicine, they give us these without holding anything back, as a mother or father would give to their child, or a friend to a friend. They give out of their great means. They will give to us according to our needs, and they will give to us as much as we can receive. Their wish for us includes both the relative, provisional, day to day needs, and also those things that are of ultimate benefit, such as teachings and encouragement, and good conditions for spiritual growth. Their love and their kind wish for us is of one nature.

I heard someone give the definition of blessing, in the Buddhist sense, as that which removes obstacles to spiritual practice, which I think is a good definition because it includes both relative and ultimate things.

Making a distinction – the word 'deity'

If I had to choose one term that isn't translated well from Eastern culture to Western culture, it is the word 'deity'. More often than not, translators are not communicating the intended meaning. The reason is this: whether or not we identify with the Western religious traditions, as Westerners we have ideas about God as part of our culture. We have all these associations, automatically, for the word God and its synonyms that, in this case does not apply. When trying to understand what words are referring to that come from non-theistic cultures, some effort is needed to get at a clear sense of their meaning.

We can say for certain that Buddhism does not make use of the idea of a creator God, all powerful, and all knowing. It does however have teachings, and it does make use of practices that call upon and access what can be called 'help from the other side'. There is calling upon beings that help.

When Tibetan teachers speak in English, sometimes they don't translate the word 'yi-dam', and they explain it as keeping the bodhisattva – divinity 'held tightly in the mind', as a method of meditation, as a path, and as a means of benefit.

A first level bodhisattva, in some teachings, is described as having at least the experience of insight into the cause of the end of suffering, that freedom and joy. And Buddhist teachings on what is called refuge tell us that if someone or some being is still subject to suffering or change, then that is not a reliable source of protection in the long term. We should seek true refuge, true and lasting protection and support. This, in Buddhist teachings, is what distinguishes Buddhas, or enlightened beings as true refuge.

Perhaps, rather than use the word 'deity', sticky, or perhaps misleading as it is, I would propose the term 'divinity' – since we do have the idea that the sacred can be here in this world; that it is here for us, available, and to be received with deep respect. The sense of divinity can be cultivated and awakened throughout our lives.

One more thought: regarding a question such as 'Where is Tara?' We usually divide the world up in our thinking in ways it is not actually divided. We say there is an inside and an outside to our life. Looked at energetically though, the so-called inside and outside are one.

If we think of Tara as an archetype, an aspect of the universal soul we all share, this can have connotations of being purely something inside. My sense is that it's truer to say that Tara, and the other Buddhas, Saints, or Bodhisattva Sangha exist in the realm of one-ness, where the inside and outside are both included, where they are one. I think this accounts, at least in part, for the effectiveness of these methods.

A note on the prayer that follows:

I usually don't comment on anything I write out that is more lyrical, since these sorts of things should speak for themselves, but in this case maybe it would add something to say the following.

I had the idea that describing a bodhisattva, or a guardian or benefactor can be likened to talking about a person. We may say the person has this quality, or likes to go here or there, or spend their time like this, all of which would be for the sake of trying to give us some idea of the person. All the different things we could say would be to introduce us to the essence of the person. So it is with this poem about Tara. The different aspects or qualities mentioned refer to something that is one essential nature – that is Tara. The purpose of writing this, and reflecting on it is to get in touch with what is being talked about.

One more thing may be worth mentioning. While much of this is very personal, I've been surprised to learn that others have had similar experiences with Tara. And so here I am writing this out this prayer and sharing it with others, with the hope that it brings others, my dear friends and family, the same, and greater, benefit.

In Praise of Tara

Holy Tara, Protector of living beings,
May your blessings flow throughout all of our lives
and by Your Compassionate Activity,
may all the myriad needs of all the myriad beings
be completely fulfilled

Tara
Your beauty tames the minds of living beings.
You draw all beings to yourself.
Your virtue calms their fears and brings them all fresh
happiness.

You are the one who makes what seems to be the impossible
entirely possible
You conquer disbelief, and dispel doubt
without leaving even a trace
You are miraculous activity, beyond comprehension.

You are 'swift to regard', quick to respond,
the remover of obstacles.
You are our protector
You are grace and blessings,
the relative and ultimate liberator of beings

Your beauty inspires uprightness of moral character
You pacify habit energy
We shed our skins, lose our old ways,
like leaves falling off of trees

You bring new birth, and give new strength
You purify the mind - like the stream-clearing jewel

You uplift and brighten the mind

For those with positive aims,
You are their Great Benefactress

You set all things right
You bring about reconciliation without impediment
without anything blocking it
You bring harmony to every surrounding circumstance

You help us to gather all positive conditions
You bring out the best that is in us all
You make all practices effective
It has always been this way
It is this way now
It will always be this way

You are the spring-like feeling of 'yes',
the sum of all optimism,
joyful positive energy,
the feeling of 'I can'

Tara,
May your blessings completely illuminate all of our lives
and may all the myriad needs of all the myriad beings
be completely fulfilled now

O, Bright Virtue!
You are light
You are grace in my life
and subtle nourishment
The blessing of all the women who have ever wished me well

You are instinctive love,
all-accommodating
naturally inclusive
comprehensive

You are embodied enlightened intelligence,
intuitive awareness, the heart awake,
and the flourishing of joy

You are playful, youthful, joyful, quick, charming, elegant,
inspiring, wise, warm, strengthening, encouraging, healing,
calming, stabilizing;

How can I call you? Tara - hope, positive energy, joyful, pure,
wholesome energy

With your rivers
nurture my limbs, these fields
With your warmth, your light
bring about the total flowering of goodness…

Tara,
May your blessings be established in all of our lives

Because this is Divine Feminine energy, quick to respond
with magical activity,
the equivalent of the patron saint of lost causes,
grace,
spiritual beauty bringing light, giving hope,
removing obstacles,
calming fear, pacifying suffering,
and protecting
bringing harmony to every surrounding circumstance,

bringing life, health, happiness, good fortune, and stability

and, being the Spring-like sum of all optimism, inspiring,
positive energy,
enabling all the good things we would do to become effective,
to become fulfilled,
to become complete,
This is called Green Tara
May all share in these blessings...

Notes on Ritual

{Most of what I've written here are not the kinds of things that are talked about often, even with friends. Nevertheless, I've enjoyed sketching out these ideas, and I thought that maybe others would also find something useful or interesting in them.}

1. Ritual is closely associated with magic, and so it may be helpful first to give my working definition of magic, as I've come to understand it. Magic is the art of bringing about changes in the outside world, by changing something on the inside, or in our consciousness. When you look at rituals around the world, and in different times, they all have this in common. In fact, with this definition, we begin to see magic in many places where that term is not usually associated, such as in a church service, at a baptism, ordination, or initiation; at a wedding, or at a concert.

Here are a couple of quotes on the subject by Colin Low, from Ritual Theory and Technique:

"...ritual is a means to an end, the end being the deliberate manipulation of consciousness

"...magical power comes from the conjunction of a symbol and a person who can bring that symbol to life, by directing and limiting their consciousness through the symbol

"Magical power comes from the person or people, and not from the superficial trappings of ritual...

"The key to ritual is the manipulation and shifting of consciousness"

"A characteristic of magical consciousness which distinguishes it from normal consciousness is that in most magical work the

magician moves outside the "normally accessible" region of consciousness."

2. Intention

A ritual starts with forming an intention, and then uses symbols, objects, sounds and words to achieve a shift in the consciousness of the director of the ritual, such as a priest or priestess, as well as the participants and observers of the ritual. All the actions, objects used and parts of the ceremony have this one simple aim.

I heard of one ritual that took a year to plan. When my friend was explaining this, to my delight, I understood right away why such a ceremony would likely be effective: so much of the thought about the purpose of the ritual would be present, along with all the energy put into it to that point.

It's useful and important to bring our best intentions to any ritual we may do, and that it is done, as they say, in the spirit of 'in the best interest of all, according to the free will of all'. This keeps it from accessing or activating and amplifying any of our regressive, or the more base human tendencies, such as greed, or aggression. Having an open heart, a good, human heart, and a generous spirit serves both ourselves and our ceremonies well.

3. The nature of consciousness vis-à-vis ritual

We can learn that consciousness always has creative effects. We can even say that every state of consciousness is creative, and that we are creating our reality all the time, but we don't usually notice this. One of the lessons I took away from the study of magic and ritual and the Western Esoteric Traditions was just this: that we are continually creating our life as we experience it.

4.

Why ritual then? The purpose of ritual is to facilitate the particular changes or the conditions we would seek. It is also a more concentrated form of what we are doing all the time – invoking forces, bringing power down through the planes to accomplish our ends. For this reason, we should be as clear as possible about what we want from a ritual.

Another reason for ritual is that we are also, most of us at least, usually subject to what is called 'mundane views' in Buddhism – that is to say, although we may say we believe in the existence of Saints and Saviors, the beneficence of Guardians and Protectors, in our usual thinking we are without much, if any faith or trust or firm belief. Ritual is a way of affirming these deep truths – that we are not alone, and that we are protected, guided and helped by Angels and Ancestors, by all of the forms, seen and unseen, of the Divine.

5.

Ritual can be simple or complex, and this is really a personal matter. There is also a balance to be achieved. Once we understand what is going on, and what is being aimed at, we can tailor a ritual to suit our own preference and needs. Sometimes I like to read or recite the traditional prayers, and add my own. Sometimes gathering offerings feels delightful, and sometimes I recognize that a ritual may be entirely on the level of mind.

Most Wiccans would perhaps disagree, seeing as they seek to ground or embody the fruits of their practice on the physical level, but I think it's only a slight shift in perspective that I'm referring to here. The fruits of our inner work should certainly. have its effect on the level of earth, but I've come to think that this happens quite naturally, in its own time and manner.

6.

The elements of a constructed ritual can include such things as: the time and place being planned ahead of time; bathing, putting clean clothes on; music, incense, flowers and fruit, colors and images or statues, and perhaps an outline of prayers or invocations, calling on the particular form of the divine for purposes that have been agreed on ahead of time.

Any ritual makes use of what are called 'correspondences', which is to say that we gather ingredients of a like nature together, the sun and stars and images of heroes, the color red and triumphant music, to gather courage, for example. The Tree of Life, or Kaballah, as it is taught and practiced in the West, has extensive lists of correspondences for various purposes, if a person is interested. See Dion Fortune's The Magical Kaballah.

7.

Ritual can be a beautiful thing, an inspired creation. We are encouraged to get creative with it, within the bounds of what is effective, and this isn't so hard to do, after all.

A place should be made in the ceremony for improvisation, to allow for inspiration in the moment, as this often will be a sign and then a furtherance of the shift in consciousness that is sought and accomplished in a good ritual.

8.

There is always concentration involved, and, if the ritual is a lovely and inspired thing, then concentration happens very naturally, like a river flowing.

9.

Ceremony should be a balance between reverent and relaxed. A sense of humor is not at all out of place, but we should aim at something elevated, overall.

10. A Ritual has a clearly defined intention, time and place

The time can be decided with the help of astrology, looking for compatible signs or planetary conditions for what we would accomplish. For example, the beginning of a waxing moon is good for rituals of increase, gathering energy, health, resources or wisdom; waning moons are good for releasing, transitions, letting go, preparing for a new phase.

When the energy flows in, astrologically speaking, it's a good time for reflection, and when it moves outwards, it's in accord with expansive rituals with an expansive purpose.

At times, there is no choice but to do a ritual of a certain nature, even though the astrological influences are not in accord, or are even in opposition. If this can be avoided, that's best, but when it can't, even though it's likened to swimming or rowing against the current, we can take that in to account. I recall one teacher saying that at times when the conditions were not right, energetically, sometimes it is best to 'tack back and forth' and to wait until the tide and time changed.

Mostly though conditions can be worked with, through the strength of the mind and intention and the divine forces that are always available to help.

11.

Rituals, simple or complex, usually have a clear start and end. This is to keep the energies of the different levels of our experience from 'intruding' or being not controlled outside of a ritual setting, or our will.

Someone once said that meditators in the East condition their consciousness to perceive and access more subtle levels of reality, whereas Westerners in general used ritual to 'amplify' the same forces for their benefit. Either way, there is a start and an end to ritual, in come cases 'opening the circle' and giving the invited forces license to depart, or to remain and help if they would do so. Actually beginning a ritual can be as simple as lighting a candle or ringing a bell, with the intention to begin, and the conclusion can be putting it out, ringing the bell again, and getting up to resume our day.

12. Place – Magical Space

There is in many rituals, a designation of the space, marked with borders of some kind, such as stones or sand, or objects. This can be cleansed, or treated in a special manner, burning purifying incense such as sage, sprinkling blessed water or ocean water, and arranging flowers and an altar. Like a church or temple, this circle or consecrated space is the 'container' so to speak, where the energy can be gathered for a purpose. It is used and then at the end of the ceremony the thoughts about it are dissolved, or 'opened'.

"A sacred circle has several purposes, the most significant of which is to define an area where formal ritual work can be performed. A circle is a place in which the rules and conditions are different to that of the everyday world. A magic circle is to contain any magical energy raised and to prevent its dissipation until it has been used up is another purpose of the circle. It is also your protective space. The sacred circle does not need to be physically represented (drawn or marked on the ground), it just needs to be visualized. In other words, you will be creating a "virtual circle"." - Puzuzu

The circle is used and then at the end of the ceremony dissolved, or 'opened'. The space is cleared, and the ceremony is completed, finished. Things are put away. For practical purposes, such a delineation is made between our ritual work and our everyday lives.

In truth, we are multi-dimensional beings, with all kinds of resources, but we don't usually recognize ourselves as such.

As I understand it these days, eventually we can function on different levels simultaneously, without it being a distraction or confusing. Until then, simply as help to keep things in order, we begin and end accessing the inner dimensions consciously.

13.

To transition back to our everyday, and now more enlightened and blessed state of consciousness, it's a good idea to do some form or celebration for a time, such as a sharing of food. When we transition slowly and deliberately, it brings more of the energy of the ritual or the meditation into the rest of our lives, and when we want more of that energy, we can reference that feeling again, and access it as needed.

14.

In the East and in the West, they say that some things are self-revealing, and this is certainly true of magic, the power of the word, visualization, prayer, ritual, and ceremony. We may think we know what we, and the forces we are surrounded with and upheld by are capable of, but we never really know what is possible until we engage them and we see for ourselves. Even then, we're likely to forget, living our lives in the world, and so a regular practice of ritual does more than accomplish a particular aim. More importantly it reminds us of who we are, and the heritage we do all have by grace, and by the blessings of all the benevolent forces of the universe.

In summary, the elements of constructing a ritual, in three general parts are:

the preparation:
forming the intention for what we would do as clearly as possible planning the place and time, gathering the materials, food, flowers and fruit, incense, prayers, etc.

creating the physical space – placing objects around the participants, visualizing and bringing to mind that this is being done with a purpose

the actual ritual:

a physical start can be done by a gesture, such as lighting candles or ringing a bell a set number of times; beginning with a statement of what is aimed for, invoking blessings, and praying for whatever assistance is needed

reflection, song, prayers or meditations can then be used to bring to mind and to the ritual the source of blessings; this can go on for as long as one wishes, or until the ceremony reaches its natural fullness

and the conclusion:

making clear in some way that the ritual is completed, perhaps with a statement of thanksgiving to that effect; dismissal of visiting forces, or the invitation for those blessings to remain available; taking apart any physical arrangement that has served its temporary purpose;

celebration and transition back to normal, and now more blessed consciousness and life

On Mysticism

Meister Eckhart said, *"God is a great underground river,"* and the
wisdom in all religions taps into this one source. – Matthew Fox

We must all become oceans now,
deep at that,
and as broad

There is a passage in a short biography of Inayat Kahn that
reads as follows:

*'Inayat began to teach and discuss his world view with different
people who would ask what to call this mode of thought. For a long
time, Inayat refused to give it a name fearing it would create barriers
between people. He would say only it was ancient wisdom from the
one and only source.*

*'He emphasized how none of the great spiritual teachers gave a name
to their religious views. Finally, knowing that a body of thought
needs some identifier to unify it, he told people it was Sufism.'*

The World Today Needs More Mystics

A mystic is someone who has taken their spiritual path far
enough to see the universal truth of it. This gives them an
understanding of other traditions, not in terms of their history
or doctrines, but from the point of view of their goal.

They have reached 'the one without a second'. Now, isn't it just
this depth of realization that is so needed in the world today?
This is what enables people to give up their exclusive claim to
the truth.

'Truth is one, but people call it by different names' – The Rg Veda

Think of all the wars in history that have been carried out in
the name of religion – in all of these, people felt that they
alone knew the will of God, or Allah, and that everyone else
was a threat and needed to be converted or die.

One of the great world scriptures, the Bhagavad Gita has this remarkable exchange on the subject of narrow mindedness that has stayed with me since I first read it more than twenty years ago. It goes like this:

Someone asked a wise person, what is the most amazing thing in the world?, and the wise person answered, the most amazing things are two: first, that all around us, people are dying, and yet we think that we will never die, and second, that everywhere, people think that others are fools, and that they alone have the truth. !

I've brought this to mind many times over the years, to try to pry open my mostly unconscious grip on ideas, to try to let some light and fresh air in. It is so on the mark, I'm happy to say, I think it's worked more often than not!

Think of all the close minded arrogance there is in religion today, and all of the fear and mistrust of others. All of this comes, not from religion or spiritual practice itself, but from a lack of depth, from a lack of realization within those very traditions. The traditions themselves are all perfectly capable of producing saints – what's lacking is profound understanding.

We so live surrounded on all sides by a sea of ignorance of other beliefs, and intolerance, that most of us take it for granted. We seldom look, or ask how other faiths can be seen and profitably understood.

The closest we may come to getting a glimpse of how pervasive intolerance is in these times, is when we see the sectarian divisions within religions themselves. Sometimes these are the most antagonistic – the most famous these days probably being the Catholic-Protestant divisions in Ireland, but there are others that I know about closer at hand.

For example, when one the followers of a Buddhist teacher disagrees with another person who is being taught within the same lineage, you can be sure they don't even regard other schools of Buddhism as genuine, or as being worthy of respect and consideration, let alone study.

And if this is the case within one school, then other religions are not even viewed as anything other than mistaken. Their perspective, time honored and filled with saints in their history, nevertheless, at the very least, is not received at all. And never mind those who have no religious affiliation – they are not even registered as having anything of truth and genuine worth to offer to humanity. And remember, here we're just talking, thankfully, about the most benign form of intolerance. At the very least, there is an absence where there could be a greater flourishing of understanding, learning, and even practice.

This kind of extreme, closed minded sectarian thinking is there in American Christianity, and in Islam too, and I'm sure in other religions as well. Narrow minded intolerance everywhere has the same characteristics, and what a loss it is to us all!

The problem of idolatry

Every religion has recognized the danger of mistakenly worshipping what is not the real source of benefit to ourselves and others. This may be like seeing a tree, but not seeing its roots.

In the Old Testament the idol was 'the golden calf'. In the Book of Mark, Jesus says, 'I will destroy this temple, made of hands, and, in three days, build another, made without hands.'

Further on in that same Book, it says:

'… and the veil of the temple
was torn from top to bottom…'

Islam, to this day, has a prohibition against any representation of the Ultimate truth. And the Zen Buddhist Tradition, throughout its teachings, is especially keen on exposing the limitations of language, and where we get caught by forms.

In the account of what is regarded as 'the first Zen discourse', the Buddha, without speaking, simply held up a flower. Only Mahakasyapa saw the Buddha's intent, and he smiled. The Buddha then said, 'I have a treasure of insight that I have transmitted to Mahakasyapa.'

Thich Nhat Hanh commented that, while everyone was wondering, what is the deep philosophical meaning, only one person saw. When someone holds up a flower, well, he wants you to see it. {a paraphrase, as best as I remember it}

'Build me a seamless monument', they also say in Zen. Go beyond the words, and then go beyond the going beyond, i.e., don't be attached to that either.

It is, as I have heard Meister Eckhart express it, that, 'as long as we love any image we are doomed to live in purgatory.' {i.e., as long as we're thinking this way, we're only half way there}

But forms alone are not the problem. The crux of whether some form of worship is idolatry is the extent to which we have penetrated the meaning of the symbol. If we have not, that very act sets us up against every other symbol, and every other form of worship. If we have, we find ourselves in deep accord with them all.

We should all be offering each other our best gifts, but instead, because of limited understanding and our attachment to forms, the door is shut and barricaded before our guests even turn up the lane! We go to war against our brothers out of that very same narrowness of view.

Here's part of a poem:

We must all become oceans now,
deep at that,

and as broad
anything less
and the light that could feed,
and save us,
instead
turns against us

Religions become most dangerous forces when they are not fully understood, when we don't penetrate to their universal depth. They can rouse natural devotional passion, and instead of that illuminating reason, and people's lives, and the world, that same ardor can go in terribly wrong directions, as evidenced by so much of what's in the news this last decade and more.

Maybe once long ago, and until recently, people could survive, and even thrive holding to one perspective, one teaching, one teacher and tradition. It may have been that there was no need to understand other faiths, as people either didn't come into contact with them, or else they were not dependent on them in any way.

Although I would argue that their lives would have been enriched, and wars based on misunderstanding would have been avoided had people actually learned in some depth, and with respect, what others believed, still it may have been possible somewhere for people to live in peace and fulfillment with secure in just their one set of beliefs.

But these times we are living in now are different. In our increasingly globalized world, we are confronted more and more, whether we like it or not, with different faiths, different languages, different poetics, and different tellings of history. The one thing we can't do any longer is to ignore that there are other traditions.

At this time, we can either choose to attach even more firmly to our beliefs, and, with even greater fervor and intensity, deny any validity other than that, which fundamentalists everywhere are doing, or we can go in the opposite direction and begin to open to the possibility that truth itself is not just contained in one tradition or set of beliefs. In other words, we can become more realized in our own tradition, and to some extent at least, in our own way, touching universal truths, we can become mystics.

As each day goes by, the need for mystics grows more and more. We need people who have taken the practices of their tradition far enough so they recognize the same essential truth shining in those who walk other paths. More and more, we need people who will spread this truth about the religions of the world.

In the past, it may have been enough to just produce realized beings who had no contact with or knowledge of other traditions. In these times though, it's a dangerous thing not to understand that our own path aims to bring us to a goal shared by others.

Add to religions devotional passion the contact with other traditions, without understanding this truth, and this is exactly how fanaticism comes about. People blow up buses, clinics, open fire in churches, burn mosques, and deny that we are all of one family, all out of this kind of blindness.

What we need is a depth of realization, produced everywhere, in all traditions and non- traditions, such as the arts, that sees the universal truth of our own particular path, and that then goes on to embrace all of humanity, all of life as its own, naturally encouraging others to do the same.

We need to reach beyond distinctions, 'where there is neither East nor West'.

Rabindrath Tagore offers us these timeless lines:

'O, grant me the prayer
that I may never lose the bliss

of the touch of the One
in the play of the many'

and,

'Where the mind is without fear,
and the head is held high,
where knowledge is free;
where the world has not been broken up
into fragments,
by narrow domestic walls –
into that heaven, wake!'

When you look at mystics across time and cultures, it's reassuring to see how they have more in common with each other than with many of their fellow believers.

'All mystics', said Saint-Martin, 'speak the same language and come from the same country.' They all teach that life is sacred, and that the highest ideal is love. They all affirm that life is one, and that, whoever we are, wherever we are, we belong to that one life, and to each other.

Twentieth Century theologian Howard Thurman wrote, in The Luminous Darkness,

"It may be, I don't know, that to experience oneself as a human being is one with experiencing one's fellows as human beings. It means that the individual must have a sense of kinship to life that transcends and goes beyond the immediate kinship of family or the organic kinship that binds him [or her] ethnically or "racially" or nationally. He has a sense of being an essential part of the structural relationship that exists between him and all other men [and women], and between him, all other men [and women], and the total external environment. As a human being, then, he belongs to life and the whole kingdom of life that includes all that lives and perhaps, also, all that has ever lived. In other words, he sees himself as a part of a

continuing, breathing, living existence. To be a human being, then, is to be essentially alive in a living world."

Isn't it clear now more than ever, with all our differences emerging, that this view what we need more of? This is what will harmonize the differences, and make the cacophonous discord of Babel a great ocean-like symphony, enriching to us all.

Other mystics come to mind here, such as Rumi, Hafiz, Meister Eckhart, Hazrat Inayat Kahn, Lama Yeshe, Thich Nhat Hanh, Albert Schweitzer, Martin Luther King, the poets Mary Oliver, Naomi Shihab Nye and Pablo Neruda, and of course the Buddha, and Jesus.

There are greater and lesser mystics, people with deeper or less profound realization, but we do need them all.

It is also entirely possible for someone to reach a depth in their practice without thinking of it as mysticism. Seeing a unity behind the multiplicity of forms, depends on contrast, which goes like this:

Whether someone recognizes that they've found a unifying truth depends on whether they come in contact with other language and methods, and, in an open-hearted, open minded way comparing their tradition with his own, he sees with joy that they come to the same conclusion.

Part of it, certainly, is having the intention to look. There can never be a legacy-tradition of realized beings, passed down like so many physical goods, for this reason. We each need to affirm certain truths for ourselves. But when we see the need to look deeply, the same truth we find within also begins to be seen elsewhere, to shine from other sources.

I recently had the surprise and delight to hear the following, expressed by Father Thomas Keating:

'If one completes the journey to one's own heart, one will find oneself in the heart of everyone.'

How wonderful!

Rabia has a poem also, in which she says:

'In my soul
there is a temple, a shrine,
a mosque, a church
where I kneel.
Prayer should bring us to an altar
where no walls or names exist...'

If we see this much it should be enough.

It is clear to me on my good days that traditions have these two aspects to them, the precious historical dimension, and the ultimate dimension, which goes beyond any one tradition, and that empowers all traditions. Recognizing the aspect that is beyond names and forms, then we know at that time our unity with other people, in other places and Faiths.

It is this ultimate dimension that gives life to traditions, both our own, and those of others. It's like when the roots of a tree go down deep into the earth and reach water, and that life nourishes the whole tree. Then all the branches, leaves, flowers and fruit will certainly flourish.

It has always been this way in the past, it will always be this way in the future, and it is this way now.

How to pray, How to act, and How to live in this world

The strength of devotion, and the joy of believers in the different traditions tells us that they have each found a source of strength and sustenance, and that they know keeping in contact with that is essential for their spiritual survival and continued strength.

One of the great things about being alive in these times is that we have so many choices of teachings and teachers available to find what meets our needs, our karmic affinities, and character. I have no doubt that anyone who searches sincerely, without giving up will find the living water.

It gets so personal at that point, and it never need be anything other than that. Think of a rose, or a pine tree, or a wave - they can only be what they are, thankfully. It's in being what we are made to be that we give our gift fully to this world.

A version of 'think globally – act locally'

I remember being surprised a number of years ago, when I went to receive acupuncture treatments, to find out how they can place a needle in one part of the body, to effect another. I remember this now because it seems to be exactly analogous to what we would think of as acting locally.

The truth of it is that, just like the body is one, this life is one, and anything we do on a personal level, even the smallest action, effects the whole of life. We may not see it, but we can be sure that it is so.

Wherever we are in life then, as long as we are acting with a positive motivation, with kindness and compassion, and being as inclusive as we can, we can be sure that life beyond what we see benefits.

We can continue to learn throughout our whole lives, and share what we know, and the basis for doing this will always be the depth of our own spiritual practice and insight. This aspect of living must be honored, my brothers and sisters, in all its forms.

Our eyes and our heart are privileged to see many of the ways people live, and believe, and practice their path today. Even if we don't understand the language, or what they do, or if we see them practicing their path only partway, still the common basis of our faith and life can always be clear to us, and constant. And, life with all its challenges, at that point, as the mystics love to tell us, is fulfillment, a great festival of celebration, and of service.

Hafiz says:

You carry all the ingredients
To turn your existence into joy,
Mix them,
Mix them!

and

We have not come here to take prisoners
Or to confine our wondrous spirits,
But to experience ever and ever more deeply
Our divine courage, freedom, and
Light!

and

You are with the Friend now
And look so much stronger.
You can stay that way
And even bloom!

Keep squeezing drops of the Sun
From your prayers and work and music
And from your companions' beautiful laughter.
Keep squeezing drops of the Sun
From the sacred hands and glance of your Beloved
And, my dear,
From the most insignificant movements
Of your own holy body.

Now, sweet one,
Be wise.
Cast all your votes for Dancing!

A mysticism of personal and collective value

I know that when many people read lines such as these they think, 'what does this have to do with my life?' Spirituality in general, and mysticism in particular have gotten a bad rap over the years as having nothing to do with life in the world, and as having little or nothing to offer, but nothing could be further from the truth.

Who among us is actually able to bear witness, and to respond to suffering effectively, other than people who are liberated from their own inner conflicts, in other words, those who have matured far enough in their spiritual life. This maturation can take any form, but everywhere it is the same story unfolding, wherever there is an effective method at work – born of empathy, then, by their fruits we know them.

Ralph Waldo Emerson wrote:

"Place yourself in the middle of the stream of power and wisdom which animates all whom it floats, and you are without effort impelled to truth, to right and perfect contentment. Then you put all gainsayers in the wrong. Then you are the world, the measure of right, of truth, of beauty. If we would not be mar-plots with our miserable interferences, the work, the society, letters, arts, science, religion of men would go on far better than now, and the heaven predicted from the beginning of the world, and still predicted from the bottom of the heart, would organize itself, as do now the rose and the air and the sun."

What mystics especially have to offer, in addition to being able to respond with wisdom to the lives of those around them, is an understanding of our common ground, that we are all of one family, and that it is our responsibility and privilege, the greatest joy for us, to care for one another. It is this universal perspective, a unitive vision, and active engagement in healing the world soul, that truly characterizes the mystic, and not those caricatures imagined from a distance.

Addressing an unfounded bias against spiritual practice, Matthew Fox, the author of Original Blessing, was asked the following question about the place of the mystic in society:

Sam Keen: 'It seems to me that psychotherapy, like religion, is concerned with healing and that it has the virtue of providing a time and place for remembering our individual wounds and for private lamentation. But don't both fail to lead us beyond our private suffering and into the wounds of the body politic?'

and he replied: 'Both therapists and politicians should join the mystics in leading us, gently but surely, into the wounds of our times, because if we did not live in such denial we could develop the collective imagination necessary to deal with our problems. But we are afraid to face the nothingness.

'The mystics tell us that from the encounter with nothingness comes a breakthrough into imagination and creativity -- the next step in the journey. Once you experience the awe and face the darkness, creativity is unleashed. It's not something you have to manufacture. Creativity is utterly natural in us. It's our divine power.

'In the final stage of the journey, creativity gives us the impulse and power to transform ourselves and our society. I think of the transformative way as the practice of compassion, the struggle for healing, for justice, for bringing the balance back into our bodies, our psyches and our communities.'

Acting this way, always and everywhere, we are taking part in something larger than ourselves, 'carried on the tide of the spirit', as Rumi said. There is little or nothing of the ego there, with none of the separation that comes from false distinctions.

Were the time not so pressing, I wouldn't have tried to write at this much on something so seemingly vague and impractical as mysticism. Actually, from another point of view, there is nothing more precise, and necessary in our times than pointing out how our religions have a common basis, and to try thereby to foster greater respect for other faiths.

In writing this then, it is my hope simply that enough of the great value and necessity for our times of a depth of realization and universal perspective, will have come through to encourage people on their path, for all of our sake.

May all benefit.

Interdimensionalty in Buddhism and in American Cinema

"If the doors of perception were cleansed,
all things would appear as they are, infinite..." – William Blake

In a recent movie, Tomorrowland, a young woman touches a magical medallion, and is transported to another world, where it is safe, beautiful, and enlightened. When she lets go of the button, she's back in her ordinary world. When I first saw this, I thought immediately of how it was just like the working of mantra in Buddhism – under the right circumstances, it can shift a person's awareness immediately, and produce the vision of a Pure Land that has been right here all along.

The Chan Master Hsuan Hua said, 'The ten dharma-realms are not outside of a single thought'. *'The ten dharma realms'* is a poetic way of saying *'all worlds'*. His teaching, and that of the early Zen traditions, explicitly, is that everything we experience comes from our mind.

Not everyone can see the other world in Tomorrowland, the woman's father, for example, and so, in Tantric terms, that experience has to be for the right person, doing the right practice, at the right time.

Another film that has interdimensionality as its main theme was Field of Dreams. This picture also explored the idea of another realm right here that is invisible to some, and that could be accessed and enjoyed.

A Sci-fi/horror film that also makes use of this device is The Others. A few more are The Lake House, Ghost, and Frequency. As with time travel movies, these films usually center around the effort of the protagonists to move between the worlds.

When we speak or write or make movies about inner realities, it's very easy to impose the laws of the physical universe. We talk for example of deeper levels of consciousness as if there were *some distance* to travel to reach the realization.

The Matrix Trilogy is perhaps the most well known series of films with interdimensionality as one of its main themes. There, you will recall, the characters have run to to make it to particular portals to pass into other places. These remind me of philosophies, or of genres in film, such as horror or those dealing with the supernatural, that seem to be second or third or twelfth hand telling of a genuine experience. People sense some truth in the story, but they are pretty far off for anyone with an experience of what we call other realms.

With ordinary thinking, we base our ideas about ourselves just on the evidence of our five senses. It is a deeply impoverished view. It's much more true to see our living here as multi-dimensional, and our identity as an inter-identity with all others. Thich Nhat Hanh calls this 'inter-being'.

What to make of all this? It is just philosophy or Science Fiction?

For more than 2,000 years, the Buddhist tradition has not only proposed an enlightened world view, but has offered ways to experience this for ourselves. The Avatamsaka Sutra, also called the Flower Ornament Sutra, is an evocative, poetic, inspiring text, presented entirely from the point of view of someone who is awake. Thich Nhat Hanh recommended that we not try to read this text like a novel, but rather that we immerse ourselves in its beauty and majestic vision.

This is what we see when we go beyond ego-grasping, with love and wisdom: the world does not disappear – far from it. We enter a Pure Land, without confusion or affliction. We experience what the Avatamsaka Sutra calls the *Entry into the Realm of Reality*.

On one retreat I attended with him in the 1990's, Thay said, in the Avatamsaka realm, the first thing that you notice is that there is a lot of light. The beings in that realm emit light, and if you are struck by one of the beams of light, you yourself begin to emit light as well. There is also a lot of space – plenty of space and time all around, as well as flowers, jewels, and lion seats, where we can sit with grace and dignity. Everything there is spoken of in terms of oceans – such as oceans of vows, oceans of peace, oceans of joy, oceans of faith, and so on... This is something we can learn to experience here and now.

He also read from chapter 36 of the text, on the Ten Kinds of Universal Penetration:

Once great enlightening beings are established in this knowledge,
they realize ten kinds of universal entry:
all worlds enter one point,
 one point enters all worlds
all beings' bodies enter one body,
 one body enters all beings' bodies
untold eons enter one instant,
one instant enters untold eons
all Buddhist principles enter one principle,
one principle enters all Buddhist principles...
untold places enter one place,
one place enters all places...
all pasts, presents, and futures enter one time frame,
one time frame enters all pasts, presents, and futures

This would be just a fantastic story, or possibility, if it were not for the compelling, suffering state of our world, with its potentially endless tragedy of delusion people experience. When we join the awareness of the pain of this world with a knowledge of its other possibilities, that are indestructibly here in everyone, a new dynamic, that of compassionate activity is set in motion.

Thay said, 'The essence of the Avatamsaka Sutra is not only insight but also a vow, an aspiration, a great determination. Avatamsaka Sutra is also action, not only wishful thinking but the will to embody deep action, action accompanied by great understanding, not a blind action.'

The truth is that it is possible for us all to access these dimensions with control, the worlds of light and peace, beauty, joy and great love. We can all draw from these as needed for inspiration and for healing.

The visionary art of Alex Grey comes as close as I've seen to representing the way things are, when seen as translucent and numinous. In Vajrayana Buddhism, we learn to see ourselves and all others like this, as essentially divine, transparent beings of light. We interact continually with others and this world, receiving blessings and responding compassionately as needed. At first we do this as an act of imagination, but gradually we learn to see that this is how things actually are, all by themselves. At that time, what we call prayer, in thought, word, and action are entirely natural.

Films such as Tomorrowland, Field of Dreams, and the Matrix offer us a clue that there are other dimensions, and something in us recognizes a truth in the telling. They can help us to begin to question our ordinary, partial perception, to begin to see, and to *free our mind*. By contrast, contemplatives, and the Buddhist traditions in particular, go much further. They assert that these dimensions are innately our birthright, each and every one of us without exception, and by teaching and example, they encourage us all to make this reality our own.

Healing the World Soul

The end of one book is always the beginning of another. We take whatever we have gathered that has been edifying, or that we think may be useful to us, and carry that forward. I'm including the following reflections here because they point in the direction I want to face, and to where I feel we need to be directing our attention and energy, to make this world a better, safer place for all our family, and for future generations. Take this as a seed then.

Healing the World Soul

Ghosts who refuse to fade away.
Ghosts we are haunted by today.
Those who demand their names and fates be recorded in the Book of Life.
Our legacies reemerging and transforming before our very eyes today.

I think of where we are also as a spiritual place. There is a level to our being here that could be called the group soul of this country. On that level, there is a great deal unanswered for, legacies that only occasionally appear in dramatic ways, but that are present in our lives, in our attitudes, in our homes and games, and diet, and economics, and education.

We are so used to thinking linearly, in simple cause and effect terms that we don't see dramatic or tragic events as related to our wars, or for example here, to this country's imperialism, and to the historical justifications for crimes. *The sum total of all that is latent violence in us manifests in countless ways*, but we see only a part, respond to even less, and collectively accumulate more fear and aggression.

Were we to address the source of all these forms of violence, then more than mass shootings, or our being a carceral state would be prevented. The problem is we don't ask deep questions. Our urgency hasn't translated yet into relentless, focussed inquiry with the aim of healing our national soul.

Beyond this one place, we are also a part of this world. Its virtues are our own, as well as all its tragic histories. Were we to reach deep into out national psyche, we would find wellsprings of thought, and sources of strength and insight that began long before our ancestors arrived on these shores. We would also find atavistic impulses, the draw towards tribalism, exclusion, bias and learned indifference.
We carry all this with us.

Why do we act as we do? If we ask this in a superficial way, impatient to move past violence, or wars, or racism, or materialism, we'll get only a superficial, and ultimately unsatisfying answer.

If we ask this same question on deeper levels however, we find how we are made of the past, of both the wisdom and ignorance of our ancestors, the triumphs and still to be resolved dynamics set in motion long ago.

Deeper than the personal and familial, can find a national soul in us, and deeper than that, a cultural, and then a world soul as well. Healing means to heal all of these.

We begin with ourselves, with our own lives as they are now. They carry all of our past in a unique form.

We may say it was not our doing,
that this past should have no claim on us,
but the jewel box placed in our crib at birth
also has these dark mysteries
no one has ever walked in
and until it is finished
this work of revelation
will wait and will haunt us
a pressing weight that one day has to speak its name

Claiming our lives here as they have come to us is a mighty act. It means on a visceral level shedding the unspoken assertion of ourselves as individuals unconnected to our family's past, unconnected to our nation, culture, and world.

Only by going deep in contemplative practice does any of this make sense as more than an idea, or an ideal. All that needs to be healed must be addressed as both what has made us, and in the greater context of our awakened lives.

This world holds that one in its embrace

Wisdom and ignorance struggle in us, and every step forward any one of us makes benefits us all. Beyond the partial identifications, and beyond exclusion, there is a wholeness that acts dynamically in us when we sense it. This work that we are doing now, on any level we identify is really the work of healing the world soul.   Artists and parents and recluses and activists are all working, united by hidden lines of force that are made of one kind of love.

See for yourself if what I am saying is true, and it will be your truth as well.

Miracle Stories

A few true stories

The following are stories I've carried with me for years, and in some cases decades. I've never had much of a reason to write them down until now, but since I am putting together this book on the miraculous, it seems fitting to include some of these stories. In addition to what I write about in my poems, these events have certainly had a formative influence in my life and thinking, even if, or maybe because I don't fully understand what's behind them. I feel something like a weatherman standing in the rain, and saying "It's raining." I have no full explanation other than to say "there are such things in our world".

One writer on esoteric subjects, Dion Fortune, said that people would likely not believe unusual stories that don't fit into their world view, but that doesn't really matter. What is important is what they imply for our living here, and in that spirit I offer these few unusual stories, some that I've just heard about, but mostly from my own life. May they inspire more receptivity to the divine in all of our lives!

The following are not in chronological order:

Someone cut a rose
A vet's story
My Sleding incident
Meeting Swami Sivananda
Tato! (2 stories - A close call)
The raven
The 10,000 year spirit
But you are alive! (two dreams and a waking vision)
At a Garage, The Dalles, Washington, 2013

Sacre Coeur, Paris, France, 1990
Sarnath, India, 1998
A Tibetan Buddhist Healing Ritual
At a class on healing
From a seance
An inviting thought on healing - based on an experience at work
The face in the window
Tara and Amitabha - instant results - 2 stories

Someone cut a rose

When I was a teenager, I came home from school one day and my mother asked me if I had cut a rose. Apparently, someone had sent roses to my sister, and, on her dresser, one rose had been cut and laid next to the rest, which were still in their vase. My father was as work, and my mother is a devout Christian who doesn't lie. My sister was puzzled by this herself. She said later that she had been reading a book of fiction that had a passage that said the scent of roses means a deceased person's spirit was around.

A vet's story

I lived for a while with a veteran of the war on Vietnam, who was wounded there. He told me the story of having been shot, and how, as he lay bleeding from his wounds, he remembered thinking only, 'I wet the bed... I wet the bed...' He survived to tell me the story, and that, that night, his mother told him, she had dreamt she heard her son crying and saying, 'I wet the bed'.

How different this is from the usual view we can so easily have of being distant and separate from one another.

My Sledding incident

Another experience, this one perhaps more of time folding over on itself in some way, happened to me when I was maybe 15 years old. For some reason I thought it would be a good idea to try to stand up on a sled when going down a hill outside where we were living at the time. You can probably guess what happened next. I did a somersault and hit my head on the sidewalk, and needed to go to the hospital for stitches. Not so unusual so far for a teenager. But then something unusual did happen. I called a friend of mine to tell him I was going to the hospital, and the next day he told me that I had mentioned to him that I was going to see a girl there that we both knew, named Valerie Vernon. I had forgotten that I'd mentioned this to him, but I do remember him asking me, why, does she live on your street? and me saying, what? eh?, what are you talking about? I've got to go... before hanging up and going to the hospital. And Valerie was here, having her arm set in a cast, no doubt from a mis-adventure of her own.

So what does this say about time and space? Experiences like this, and the somewhat common ones of deja vu tell me that time and space exist in a way that is different from how we usually think of them – in just that consensus linear way, and as just discrete objects and places. This is something to think on, if we are to arrive at a larger understanding of time and space, and of ourselves.

"Meeting" Swami Sivananda

In the late 1980's, I house-sat for about a week for the author Piri Thomas. He had a place that was next door to the yoga center on Dolores St. One night I went to a program where they had a visiting swami who was traveling with his guru's sandals. From what I remember, part of his teaching that week was to include a ceremony on another night honoring his guru, where the sandals would be placed on the altar. I thought this was pretty funny when I heard it, but could let it pass. I thought to myself: Oh, they have the guru's sweaty gym shoes! How strange! - not exactly respectful thoughts.

There were questions from the audience after the swami's talk, and they seemed to center around this ceremony, and the sandals. The teacher was having some trouble explaining himself, and finally, out of frustration, he said, Ok, Ok, and with a gesture, Go get the sandals, go get them...

I thought then that I'd lose it laughing, and how embarrassing that would be, since I was sitting up towards the front of the packed room.

A few moments later, I felt this presence enter the room, that was warm and loving, and wise, and that knew what I was thinking, and was alright with it – in fact shared the joke with me. I turned around and there was someone at the doorway with Swami Sivananda's sandals.

In the years that followed, having studied the works of many teachers from the Indian Tradition, I've found I have the deepest connection with this same Swami Sivananda.

Tato! (2 stories - A close call)

The following two stories are from my father, and I'll let him tell them in his own words. I'll only say here that the second story he recounts was one that was well known in our family. We grew up hearing how, before any of us were born, one night on an Air Force tarmac my father had heard the voice of his grandfather calling his name. He stopped in his tracks only inches from an airplane propeller. I'd never heard the whole story until, after my father passed away, I found a document titled A Close Call, that tells a more recent story, and links it with the event from more than 50 years earlier. Here is my father's telling of the two stories:

A Close Call

It was a perfect example of how thin the barrier is from life to death. We forget that we are made of some rather mushy stuff, which cannot stand most of the powerful forces which are all around us. Therefore...

I had just dropped Marilyn off at her weekly bible session, at Laguna Honda Hospital. Coming out of their driveway, one has to make a right turn on to 7th Avenue, whereupon one has to make a u-turn at a cut-off about 100 yards down. There is a traffic light there, which I always observe, no matter if making the left turn is legal. I have the safety of pedestrians as well, who come out of the Forest Hills MUNY station. The light was red, so I stopped. When it turned green, my go, I moved my foot on to the gas pedal but, strangely, I couldn't press down.

At that instant, a pick-up went zooming by, having jumped the light. It missed me by about one foot, perhaps less. And, since the driver's side would have been hit first, I would have been toast. I froze for a couple of minutes, for I clearly knew that I had come close to either serious injury but most likely death.

Many years ago, when I was a mechanic in the Air Force, a similar situation occurred, this time with the propeller of an airplane about 6 inches from my face. I had stopped short, for I heard my grandfather's voice: "Aguántate ahi, Tato!!" "Hold it right there, Tato" (my childhood nickname). I will never forget this for my head would have been all over the fuselage of the airplane. How to explain this, unless one is a dedicated believer? I am an agnostic, closer to atheism, but I have left a small crack in the door of disbelief, for, who really knows, anything is possible, for we are severely limited with our five rather limited senses.

So, then: Could this be a repeat?? Could I have a powerful Guardian Angel keeping me safe for a purpose?? Or was I just lucky??

The raven

The last few years of my father's life, he experienced quite a few health problems, with assorted aches and balance problems, to go with some difficult emotions. My father told me this story maybe a year before he died, where he was feeling really out of sorts one day, and he looked out the window and saw a raven. He and the raven made eye-contact, and, as he told it, all his pains immediately vanished.

The 10,000 year spirit

In 1985 or so, I attended a multi-day conference on healing at Fort Mason here in San Francisco. There were teachers from many different traditions, Native American (Wallace Black Elk), Vodou (Luisa Teisch) as well as one shaman or medicine man I recall was from Africa. For some reason, I was drawn to make contact with the representatives of this particular teacher, and ask for a private consultation.

As I recall I met this person in his host's house in Marin, and told him of some of the difficulties I has having at the time, likely depression, loneliness, and such things. He offered to do a ceremony for me then and there, for a fee- maybe $200 or so, and I agreed. He said at the time he would "give me a spirit" that would "stay with me for 10,000 years". I remember that the ceremony involved his rolling a ball of herbs in his hands, and me eating it.

I went home that afternoon feeling pretty high – as in full of energy. That night I couldn't sleep, and I began to get more and more uncomfortable with the presence of the spirit I could feel. I remember thinking that it felt like there was a ceiling on how high I could reach, and that I had been given a new god, or thoughts to that effect.

I went into full response mode – remarkably when I look back on it – calling on every divine force I had ever known, and by the morning the spirit presence was either no longer there, or no longer a problem. I recall this now as my first experience of a real spiritual threat, and how it taught me that we have resources we don't know about until we need them.

But you are alive! - two dreams and a waking vision

I had a dream many years before my sister's bouts with cancer, which she has survived. In it, I was racing to find her, and I went up to a rooftop where I found her sitting. She was pregnant, and bruised, but I was ecstatic to find her. She said, Oh but look at me! and I said, Yes, but you are alive!

On hearing the second diagnosis of cancer, a year after my sister's first surgery, I went into another mode of activity. Each night I sent out a number of prayer requests before I felt like I could go to sleep. One of the spiritual centers I contacted was representing an group monasteries that had Christian nuns with a vocation to pray for others. For some reason when I heard this, I felt deeply comforted.

Shortly thereafter, my sister was visiting the store where I was working and I saw (actually more a combination of feeling and seeing) a light around her body, unlike any I had seen before. It was beautiful, and healing, and for some reason I connected it with the Sisters who were offering prayers for my sister's health.

After her second surgery, while she was still recovering in the hospital, my sister told me she had dreamed of emerging from something that went underground for a ways. I took this to represent her returning to this world for a number of years more.

At a Garage, The Dalles, Washington

Back in 2013, I had car trouble coming down from the mountains in Washington State. I made it to the first medium sized town I could, called The Dalles, and found my way to a garage that had gotten some good reviews online. The first thing I noticed when I entered was that there were quite a few Christian posters on the walls, with such things as scriptures with landscapes and images of Christ. Needing to wait around to talk to the owner, I also noticed that they were giving away some Christian literature. After getting my car looked at, I asked the owner about the religious pamphlets and art, and he told me the following story:

A number of years before, he and his partner were serious drug addicts, and he felt himself sliding deeper and deeper into a depraved lifestyle. As he told it, one day, as his partner went to use the bathroom he prayed from some deep need, and felt a brilliant, loving presence fill the whole garage. He said he knew his prayer had been answered, and that it was the Lord who was present. When his partner came out of the bathroom, he noticed that something was different in him, but couldn't tell what it was, and didn't understand the explanation. He said that, in that short time, in just those few minutes, he was completely healed. He also said that since that day he's been entirely free of addiction, and devoted to sharing Jesus and the Christian Faith.

Sacre Coeur

I visited Paris in the Summer of 1990, twenty-six years ago. While I was there, one of the places on my list to see was a church named Sacre Coeur (Sacred Heart). I remember that it was a hot day, and by the time I got there, I was feeling quite unwell. I almost gave up, especially since the church itself is on a hill, with steps leading up to it, and, being Summer, there were also a lot of other people around. But I had made it that far, and so I thought I would go in, even if it was just for a few minutes.

When I entered, I noticed that it was cooler, and more quiet, and I saw to my left that there was an alcove with a statue of Mary, and with pews set out for people to sit in. Without giving it much thought, and still feeling pretty bad, I sat down, and to my astonishment, all my discomfort immediately disappeared. I went looking for it from head to toe - nope, nothing to be found. Instead I noticed a feeling of peace and well being. As I sat there I wondered, was what I was experiencing the result of the devotion of pilgrims like myself, and their thoughts about the spiritual influence of Mary?, or was something else there? Both at that time, and looking back, I would say it was both. In times like these, there is the sense of a greater intelligence and love. I can say that I felt cared for beyond anything I could have imagined.

I think of Mary, and of Sacre Coeur with devotion to this day.

At Sarnath, India, 1998

In 1998, I visited the Deer Park, in Sarnath, India, the legendary place where the Buddha gave his first teaching. I remember it was late morning on a very hot and dry day in April, even by Indian standards. I arrived a little before noon, and entered what looked like a deserted park. There were a few ruins, mostly of stupas here and there (round monuments representing the mind of the Buddha, or a holy being), and not much else to see. Almost right away however I had a most unusual experience. I could feel my throat chakra vibrating, and I could hear it continually resonating with the syllable 'ah'. It felt like I had a small cymbal, perhaps 6 to 8 inches in diameter, that was vibrating in the area towards the front of my throat, and that was singing clear as could be.

The sound 'ah', I recognized at the time, as the syllable that represents the speech of the Buddha. I was aware of this, and also that I was at this holy place of pilgrimage, where the Founder of all the worlds Buddhist traditions first turned the Wheel of the Dharma. I walked around for perhaps 40 minutes, and all that time, my throat chakra was ringing with the sound of this sacred syllable. I was in awe of this, and fully conscious of it while it was happening.

I had had unusual experiences in temples and consecrated places before, but never as vivid and long lasting as this one.

A Tibetan Buddhist Healing Ritual

When I was traveling in Nepal, I had the opportunity to have breakfast with a well known translator of Tibetan Buddhist teachings, who enjoyed telling me some of the amazing things he'd witnessed over the years. Here is one of the stories I remember hearing from him:

Once there was a young man who had a severe case of boils all over his face and body. Nothing seemed to help, and, finally, out of desperation, a relative brought him to see a Tibetan Lama. After looking into the matter through a method of divination, the Lama said that this kind of problem was caused by tree spirits that had been angered for some reason, perhaps because of being urinated on, and suggested that a certain ritual be done for the young man.

Apparently, back then, there was at least one monk in each monastery who didn't eat meat, precisely for the purpose of being able to perform rituals such as this one. It involved constructing a paper-mache house, and placing it on a small raft on the banks of a stream. The monk then sang songs to the tree spirits, that had the meaning of, "Oh spirits, look at this lovely house we've made for you, Won't you come live here? Why stay in that disgusting human body? Here, you can stay as long as you like in this beautiful house we've made just for you...", and so on to that effect. After some time, with the monk continuing the song, the raft with the paper house was floated downstream.

Although at the time the young man and his relative were doubtful, a couple of days later they reported that the boils all began breaking, and soon after the problem had completely cleared up.

At a class on healing

In my early 20's I had the good fortune of meeting my first teacher, Dorothy Schlosser, at a psychic fair here in San Francisco. I soon began visiting her and her family down in Milbrae. Dorothy's husband was named Art, and he was a healer. I recall having healing sessions with him, laying on a massage table and Art either moving his hands around my body without touching it, or gently laying his hands on at various places.

I remember that, when his hands came close to my ear, I could feel a vibration and hear a tone, like a tuning fork.

About a year later perhaps, another psychic, Walter Orlinsky offered a weekly psychic development class at Dorothy and Art's place. One week was dedicated entirely to healing, and, as I remember it, from the time I arrived and for the entire 2 hour class I could hear and feel the same tone as I had heard during the healing sessions with Art. I remember that evening as being entirely blissful.

From a seance

At a seance led by this same teacher, Walter Orlinsky, a few strange things happened. One young man said he saw another fellow student shrink down to the size of a doll in her chair. My own experience was no less strange. I slowly began swaying in circles from the hips, and for some never explained reason this went on for quite a while.

The most unusual part came when Walter said he saw a young woman kicking me in the shins – and after a few moments said the name Nancy was coming to him. Nancy was the name of the girlfriend I had left behind in Maryland when I came to California a few years before. It had not been an easy parting, and I know that no one there had ever heard me mention her name.

An inviting thought on healing - based on an experience at work

One night, late in the bookstore, a young woman came in to look around. We got to talking as we walked through the aisles and she told me about a rash on her arm. As she was telling me this, I began to feel what she was describing in the same place on my own arm. I thought at the time that if I could feel her experience, then she should be able to feel my own as well.

It was just around this time that I noticed something that started out strange, but that I gradually got used to. I had a stretch of perhaps a year or more when, if I had any discomfort anywhere in my body, if I put my mind on it, I could make the pain disappear. It got so that it seemed normal, natural, and I had the thought that, of course, anyone can do this. I knew that wasn't the case, and when I could catch my mind making this into something that seemed commonplace, which even then I knew it wasn't, I would offer the prayer that others everywhere would have this same ability, to relive their own and their loved one's sufferings through the power prayer, and of directed loving kindness and compassion.

The face in the window

I worked security for a number of years, mostly by myself, but I recall once, when working with another, I came downstairs to the security station and found my co-worker drawing a face. He pointed out that a face had appeared in the fog in the window – as if someone had blown their warm breath and sketched an intricate drawing. It was still there when I looked, and I had to admit his rendition was very accurate. Sometimes visual artists, like writers, have the feeling that something, some spirit is trying to come through, and this seemed to be the case here, with the addition that the face appeared spontaneously. I have heard of such things as Buddhas faces or forms appearing in rock, so such things have been known to happen.

Tara and Amitabha - instant results - 2 stories

Once I was on a retreat, and using the office copy machine to make some copies of a Tara Sadhana, or practice text that I had found. I got most of the pages right, but when I came to the last page, for some reason, I couldn't get it straight, try as I might. I felt myself getting obsessive, trying over and over, and in a way losing control. In helplessness and desperation I called out in myself, Tara! Help! Instantly, the copy machine stopped working. When it started again a few minutes later, and after I got over the co-incidence, I got the copy straight, which at that point seemed like the lesser event.

A number of years ago, I visited Gold Mountain Monastery in Chinatown, in San Francisco. The Chinese Buddhist Tradition has a strong element of prayer and devotion to Amitabha Buddha, the Buddha of Infinite Light. They chant the Buddha's name, sometimes as Namo Amitofu, which I have also heard as Namo Amitabha Buddha -Homage to the Buddha of Infinite Light. After walking around a bit, I suddenly felt a sharp sting on my upper back. A bee had flown down the back of my shirt and had stung me. For some reason, my reaction was to say intensely to myself "Namo Amitaba Buddha!" Immediately, the pain stopped. I had been blessed, no doubt.

Poetry

A Dream to call the Angels
When I'm beaten down
Tonight I'm a lion cub in the wilderness
Imagine an underwater system of channels
prayer
Why don't we

A Dream to call the Angels

I was awake and all morning it was raining silver in my room. Gradually everything I could see became translucent, visible still in outward structure, but also clear, showing the inside, like through a membrane.

The room's light was stronger, in a soft and gentle way, than the early morning outside, and seem to come not from any one place, but to be arising evenly in myself and all that I saw. The feelings began with a dream.

I was taking a test in an ordinary over bright classroom with other young people, and everyone had a copy of the test except me. I opened my test booklet to find answers, on separate scraps of paper, to other tests. I brought the booklet to the teacher, a woman with mid-length brown hair, and she brought me back to my seat and held up something with writing on it, telling me to copy the writing down.

At first I didn't not understand, but then I came to realize that to copy this paper down constituted the whole of my test. The paper at first just looked ordinary, then it changed into an ornate colored woodcut - with fancy writing and colored pictures. It said something to this effect:

'In the late Renaissance year of 17 ? Father _____
had brought to him his charge, _____ so that he
could be nearer.
It ended with the line,
'The tutorial is completed.'

At first I thought the young person brought to the priest was some kind of prisoner, and then I realized (beginning the feeling of angels) that the young man was his student and that it was a fortunate event for all involved that the young man was being moved in closer proximity to his teacher.

In reading this over, copying it and coming to the line, 'The tutorial is completed', this bright and beautiful feeling started to rise slowly, clearly felt throughout my whole being. (I was awakened by this.)

It is an indescribable feeling of peace and well-being, pleasurable, billowing at times towards intensely so, a clarity and presence that is palpable, fixed, steady.

The presence of these spirits, angels I can only call them, brought with them gifts in the form of opening me up to certain truths that I had not seen with such a complete clarity before.

It was like being in that soft and warming glow, all over feeling of well being, opened ways of seeing.

I felt something open and began to see the fortune, the wealth of this earth that I am surrounded with. I count among these the elements of making music, of writing and learning. I count among these the people I know and am made rich by knowing, my family, also the beauty and tenderness of people I don't know as well.

I was able, am able still to see the treasure of being touched by beauty and how it waits, all this that is rich in possibility waits to be responded to with an open heart. I feel I have seldom if ever appreciated my surroundings so much. How fortunate I am!

Next, following right after this I began to see the wealth of ideas that have come through to me - I saw each of these ideas - expressed in friendship, poetry and philosophy, as if they were individuals, alive with their impulse and message, like people.

I had to ask as some point that I only be shown enough to keep my clarity. I didn't want to be overcome by the pleasurable feelings that were steadily growing.

I don't know what loosened, but these presences are quite tangible, taking up all I can see and feel, outside, inside, healing...

When I'm beaten down
and the wolves approach
the ones I guarded in my thoughts
step forward to protect me
They emerge from between the layers of my skin
They come out from my breath,
looking fierce, confident,
and they set a halo of peace around me

Tonight I'm a lion-cub in the wilderness
scratching the ground for food
crying out that I've been left alone by my ancestors
to learn to thrive if I can
I turn all my despairing out in to the night
and the air fills with the scent of my family
and I hear lion sounds
having released from this body the instinct to awaken
and the night creatures scatter…
I carry this with me, now I know
I am alone and
my whole family is with me

Imagine an underwater system of channels
one channel opens
and the stream of cool, pure water can be felt moving through
felt all the way back to its source

Contacting a spiritual tradition can be this way
the clean, clear life moving through
felt in this very place, and known to its origin
Teachers, practitioners, deities, protector spirits
virtues faithfully maintained
and given forward through lives

We are welcomed by this, our family
They are eager to assist the awakening life
the heart becomes very quiet watching this work
this far reaching, unceasing compassion

They speak behind their words
move behind the curtains of form
in silence, shaping
All of this is given to you, it is immanent
the life within the life

prayer a small candle
eclipsed by the light of day
a prompting to open the door and see who's there
a messenger announcing the arrival of the king,
medicine that grows as it's needed
with grace and comfort
least expected yet hoped for still,
against unbelief

A barren river bed offers up its cries
and stirs the core of heaven to come running
pouring itself in streams
flooding valley plains

Search out the beginning of this movement in us
to reach out, to reach upwards
and it's of the same glory as its end
like holding a small gold coin close
and passing through gates
until you arrive at a city
where everything is made of that same light…

Why don't we
invoke the blessings
of billions of angels
the light of love
to pour down upon
everyone we see,
hear, or even think of

Why don't we settle thoroughly
that we all have it in our power
to feed each and every one
with the food that matches their deepest
need and desire
and then do it

Why don't we do this?
It costs us nothing if we do
and costs us all so much if we don't

Why don't we
wash the feet of all weary travelers,
offer them humble sustaining fare
and a soft bed
for them to be able to continue
laden with gifts
on their way

Why not
spread lotus blossoms
on the ground for each person to walk on
every step of their way

Why don't we

Why don't we
wash away the murk
of our own confused thinking
and so stand resplendent
and as light for everyone's eyes

Why don't we pick up
in both our precious hands
that part of the wounded staggering
world soul
we've each been given
to restore to health

In this, the briefest of moments,
this brief meeting,
our being here together,
O now,
Why don't we cup
in our hands
the dreams of future generations
and heal all injury
as our gift to be passed forward in time

I say,
Why don't we
abide in perfect, overflowing fullness
with every gift passed around
from one house to another
no limit

all the broken
isolated
born but not able to be fully born –

this, plus the heart
and there is vow
this path made entirely of
somehow wanting,
needing to say
a mighty yes

About the Author

Jason Espada is a writer and classical musician living in San Francisco. He is a steward of his father's photography, and the founder of abuddhistlibrary.com. Over the years, he's made a number of recordings of Buddhist teachings, and these days his focus is on the connection between spirituality and social action. His new website is jasonespada.com.

Also by Jason Espada

Living in Beauty - Buddhist Loving Kindness Practice begins with traditional teachings on how we can cultivate metta, or loving kindness, starting from wherever we are now in our lives. This love is the basis for what is known as the Bodhisattva Vow, which is the aim to benefit others as much as we can through actualizing a spiritual path. Metta then finds expression through Engaged Buddhism.

In an era of increasing isolation, materialism, fear and despair, metta helps us to tap into our inner richness, and gives us reason to hope. For this reason, metta is the ideal practice for our times.

A Buddhism for Racial Progressives - Inspiration for Activists is a handbook on Buddhism and social justice. It presents a compassionate world view, and methods that can help us to achieve our aims. Using traditional teachings, we have greater resources to bring to the work that we do.

Ending Racism - A Buddhist View is a response to the ongoing crisis in this country of systemic discrimination and police violence. It details what Buddhism can teach us about the deep education that needs to take place to remove the roots of racism in our culture.

Where Joy Can Be Found is about the happiness that is essential for each of our flourishing. We may think of joy as a luxury, as something we can get only when we're finished with our day to day tasks, or after achieving some goal. The reality is that we need this quality that enlivens all throughout our life, if we're going to bring out the best we have in us.

A Practice that Thrives in Difficulty - Buddhist Thought Training describes methods for turning adverse circumstances into causes of healing and awakening, so that instead of being oppressed by conditions, we can be empowered by them. When things are especially difficult in our lives and in our world, compassion can manifest even more strongly. The Thought Training teachings then show us how we can use everything we meet to benefit both ourselves and society.

Poetry

The Life Within the Life

Shadows and Exiles - Made to Receive All the World

Original Waters

Be a light in the gathering light - Selected Poems

Open in case of emergency, New poems, 2017

Audio Recordings
{these can be heard on jespada.bandcamp.com/music}

1. Mahayana Prayers and Poetry

2. The Dhammapada

3. The Treatise on Buddha Nature

4. A Guide to the Bodhisattva's Way of Life, by Shantideva

5. An Exhortation to Resolve Upon Bodhi

6. The Medicine Buddha Sutra

7. The Perfection of Wisdom in 8,000 Lines, and It's Verse Summary; The Diamond Sutra, and The Heart Sutra (16 hours)

8. Selections from The Perfection of Wisdom in 8,000 Lines (one hour)

9. Dharma Readings

Music

1. Classical Guitar to Put Your Mind At Ease

2. Holiday Music for Classical Guitar

3. From the Soul of Spain

About Great Circle Publications

Great Circle Publications is dedicated to sharing the light of the world. While other circles exclude, through identifying with one tribe, nation, or religion, the qualifier, 'Great' refers to another way of living in our world; one that is inclusive, compassionate, social justice oriented, and forward looking.

Made in the USA
Middletown, DE
16 January 2020

83285284R00128